I0568522

FROM SHADOWS TO LIGHT

Reclaiming True Joy and Purpose in Your Walk With God

REV. DR. NADINE NKULU

FROM SHADOWS TO LIGHT
Reclaiming True Purpose in Your Walk with God
© 2025 Rev. Dr. Nadine Nkulu

ISBN: 978-1-969893-10-0

Cover Design: Prairie Hearth Publishing, LLC (Loretta Sorensen)
Interior Design: Prairie Hearth Publishing, LLC (Loretta Sorensen)

Unless otherwise indicated, all Scripture quotations are taken from the King James version of the bible, © 1979, 1980, 1982, 1984 by Thomas Nelson, Inc. Used by permission. All rights reserved.

Acknowledgment

God Almighty, I give all praise and glory to You for Your guidance, grace, and strength throughout this journey.

My heartfelt gratitude goes to my loving husband, Guy Nkulu, for his unwavering support, encouragement, and patience.

I am deeply thankful to my parents, Missionaries Rev. Umba and Ngoy, whose faith and dedication have been an inspiration to me and who laid a strong foundation of love and service in my life.

To my wonderful children—Nathan, Baraka, Erica, and Chrisma—thank you for your love, understanding, and for being my source of joy and motivation.

Lastly, I am grateful for the churches I serve—Wesley and Grace United Methodist Churches in Mason City, Iowa—for their spiritual guidance, fellowship, and ongoing support.

May all the glory be to God alone.

INTRODUCTION

THE SEARCH, THE SHADOWS, AND THE REAL ONE

"A wandering heart does not necessarily seek evil; it simply looks elsewhere. The more we turn our gaze away from God, the farther we drift from true fulfillment." - Rev. Dr. Nadine Nkulu

The heart of man is a seeking heart. Whether young or old, rich or poor, male or female, broken or whole, the human heart has a nature that keeps asking, keeps searching, and keeps reaching. It never wants to stay in one place too long. It wants meaning. It wants purpose. It wants to know, "Why am I here?" and, "Does this even matter?" That's why you will find people switching jobs, changing churches, moving countries, ending friendships, jumping into new ones; not because they are all unstable or unserious, but because the heart is hunting for something it cannot seem to fully grab. That search is not random. It is not baseless. In fact, it is deeply spiritual. Because whether we know it or not, that ache is the cry of a soul looking for God.

Yes, you heard that right. What we are truly looking for is not another thrill, not another title, not another compliment, and not even another answered prayer. What we are searching for is God. The real God. The Living God. The One who made us and planted eternity in our hearts.

Ecclesiastes 3:11 says,

"He hath made everything beautiful in His time: also, He hath set the world in their heart, so that no man can find out the work that God maketh from the beginning to the end."

But that word "world" as used in the above verse, in the original translation, is better understood as "eternity". In other words, God placed something eternal in your heart that cannot be satisfied by temporary things. And that is where the problem begins. Because man, in his limited knowledge, tries to feed that eternal hunger with earthly things. We try to satisfy a spiritual longing with physical pleasures. And we end up full, but not fulfilled.

Usually, the result is a Wandering heart. Moving from one thing to the next. Doing everything but still feeling like something is missing. Praying but not connecting. Serving but not satisfied. Worshiping but not feeling God's presence. Surrounded by people but still lonely. It's like standing under a shower and still feeling thirsty. You are going through all the motions of religion, but the connection is not there. Your soul is asking questions your current lifestyle cannot answer.

Psalm 42:1-2 captures this wandering cry: "As the heart panteth after the water brooks, so panteth my soul after thee, O God. My soul thirsteth for God, for the living God: when shall I come and appear before God?" Notice it didn't say "my soul thirsteth for a miracle" or "my soul thirsteth for success." No, the soul is thirsty for God, the Living God. But the issue is that, in our thirst for God, we often chase shadows that look like God.

The devil knows how to exploit that search. He knows that man is looking for God, so he packages deception in things that look good, sound spiritual, or feel fulfilling, but at their core, they are distractions. That is why Satan does not always come with horns and a red tail. Sometimes, he comes dressed as an answer. He comes as the voice that says, "Try this instead," or "God is taking too long," or "Maybe this new idea will help."

Do you remember Eve in the garden? Let us look at Genesis 3:5. The serpent said to her:

"For God doth know that in the day ye eat thereof, then your eyes shall be opened, and ye shall be as gods, knowing good and evil."

That was the lie, but it was hidden in a twisted form of truth. The devil knew Eve wanted to be like God. And the desire to be like God was not wrong. In fact, God made man in His own image. But the method to become like Him; that was where the deception crept in.

So, the serpent did not introduce a new desire. He hijacked an existing one. He took Eve's hunger for something holy and redirected it through a forbidden door. That's how many believers today end up in strange places. We didn't start off intending to drift. We just followed a voice that promised something deeper, something faster, something more exciting. We wanted more of God, but somewhere along the line, we lost track of where God actually was.

I want you to think of Saul for a moment. Of course, we know he was the first king of Israel. In 1 Samuel 13:8-14, he got tired of waiting for Prophet Samuel to arrive, so he took matters into his own hands and offered a sacrifice he was not supposed to. Why? Because people were getting restless. His heart was overwhelmed. He wanted to do the right thing, but the pressure made him take a shortcut. That's how many of us wander; we don't outrightly rebel, we simply take shortcuts in the name of "just trying to survive." But shortcuts in the Spirit often lead to long detours in destiny.

Consider Solomon, too, a man who possessed divine wisdom, wealth, and peace. Yet in Ecclesiastes 1:14, he wrote: "I have seen all the works that are done under the sun; and, behold, all is vanity and vexation of spirit." That's not a statement from a poor man. That's not a complaint from someone who lacked answers. That was the voice of someone who chased everything and still found nothing. Why? Because the heart will never be satisfied by anything less than its Creator.

And so, we see that even the wisest can wander. The most anointed can drift. The sincerest hearts can get lost along the way. But again, the devil rarely uses rebellion; he often uses distraction. That's why Paul warned us, believers in 2 Corinthians 11:3,

"But I fear, lest by any means, as the serpent beguiled Eve through his subtlety, so your minds should be corrupted from the simplicity that is in Christ."

Did you catch that? The simplicity that is in Christ. The Christian Walk is not supposed to be this complicated. But when our hearts start chasing performance, recognition, emotions, trends, or the latest spiritual movement, we move away from the simple beauty of just knowing God.

So where are we now? Many of us are stuck in the motion of religion but not the movement of relationship. We still go through the spiritual habits, but something has shifted. We feel lost, but we don't even know where we strayed. And that's what makes this so dangerous. Because spiritual wandering is not always loud, sometimes it happens silently. You don't backslide overnight. You just slowly stop enjoying prayer. You stop expecting anything from God. You still read your Bible, but nothing really speaks to you anymore. You sing songs in church, but you feel numb. You begin to lose your sensitivity to His voice. And when that numbness sets in, it becomes easier to accept substitutes for intimacy with God. That's why the devil does not attack everyone the same way. He customizes the shadow to the person. For some, he uses money. For others, he uses busyness. For others, he uses offense, disappointment, or even hurt from the church. Anything that makes you say, "Maybe I will just do this instead." And without knowing it, you are drifting; not from church, not from activities, but from God Himself.

Do you remember Demas in the New Testament? In Colossians 4:14 and Philemon 1:24, he is mentioned as one of Paul's fellow laborers. But in 2 Timothy 4:10, Paul says:

"For Demas hath forsaken me, having loved this present world…"

What happened to Demas? Was he not spiritual before? Of course he was. But something in the world called to the longing in his heart. And sadly, he answered.

Friend, the issue is not that God moved. The issue is that we did. Our hearts went on a journey, seeking meaning, answers, and satisfaction. But we wandered into shadows instead of staying in the Light. And now, here we are, looking alive but feeling empty, surrounded by noise but craving silence, doing all the right things but no longer feeling right.

THE SHADOWS VERSUS THE REAL ONE

"We are inhaling shadows and expecting them to fill us. But only the real presence of God can satisfy a real soul." - Rev. Dr. Nadine Nkulu

Even after a man has overcome the devil's first trap, that dangerous detour away from seeking God, he's still not safe. Because Satan does not stop trying just because you found the right direction. He waits again; this time not in front of you, but beside you. When the devil realizes he couldn't stop you from finding God, he changes his approach. He now tries to confuse your journey by casting shadows. He knows he cannot block the Light itself, so he stands in the way to distort it, hoping you will follow the shadow instead of continuing in the Light.

To understand this better, let's talk about shadows, not just in the spiritual sense, but from a physical and scientific one.

In physics, a shadow is formed when an opaque object stands between a light source and a surface. The light is still shining, but the object blocks part of it, and what appears on the surface is a shadow—a dark image that resembles the shape of the object, but has no substance. It's an image, but it has no life. It moves when the object moves. It is real, but it is not alive.

This is the deception the devil presents: shadows that look like Light. Activities that look like spirituality. Movements that look like revival. Knowledge that looks like truth. And while you are pursuing what looks like it came from God, your heart starts drifting again, not because you went back to sin, but because you are stuck in shadows.

Let me take you deeper into this study, because the Bible also speaks of shadows. And if we are going to walk in truth, we must explore what God says about them. Hebrews 10:1 gives us a powerful insight: "For the law having a shadow of good things to come, and not the very image of the things,…" The laws were not the real thing. It was a shadow of the real thing. In other words, they were temporary patterns meant to help men see the outline of something bigger, someone greater—namely, Jesus. But the danger is that, instead of seeing the shadows as pointers to the real, many people began to treat the shadows as the real thing. They focused on the temple, the feasts, the rituals, but missed the God those things were meant to reveal. That's what happens when the heart desires fulfillment but settles for a form. We begin to worship the shadow instead of the Light.

Let us continue that verse in Hebrews 10:1. "… can never with those sacrifices which they offered year by year continually make the comers thereunto perfect."

You can sacrifice every day, follow all the religious routines, and still not be perfected because the shadow is not enough. It may resemble something real, but it cannot change your life.

This was the same warning Paul gave the church in Colossae. Colossians 2:16-17 says,

"Let no man therefore judge you in meat, or in drink, or in respect of an holy day, or of the new moon, or of the sabbath days: Which are a shadow of things to come; but the body is of Christ."

Again, shadows. Good things. Spiritual things. But not the real substance. Christ is the real. The rest is just a pointer.

So, what are shadows in our time?

They are the things that resemble godliness but don't carry God. They are teachings that sound deep but don't point to Christ. They are the endless religious activities we engage in: conferences, events, fasting, and worship nights, which make us feel spiritual but do not bring us into intimacy with God. They are the distractions that keep us busy for God but far from God.

This is how many have gotten lost again, not in sin, but in substitutes. The enemy now tells them, "This is enough. You are doing so well. Look at your calendar. You are so active." But activity is not intimacy. Shadows don't give light; they only exist because of it. The moment you remove the true Light, shadows disappear too.

Let us return to the Old Testament and see how men clung to shadows and missed God. In John 5:39-40, Jesus says to the Jews: "Search the scriptures; for in them ye think ye have eternal life: and they are they which testify of me. And ye will not come to me, that ye might have life."

Did you catch that? Jesus was saying, "You are reading the Scriptures, but you are not seeing Me." That's how powerful shadows can be. They can blind your eyes with truth if you are not looking for the Truth, Christ.

Think about it: these people had the Law. They had the Torah. They could quote it better than anyone. Yet when the Word made flesh, Jesus, stood in front of them, they didn't recognize Him. Why? Because they had fallen in love with the form, not the Person. They had embraced the system and ignored the Savior.

It's still happening today. We have created spiritual systems that no longer need the Spirit. We know how to "have church" without Christ. We have learned the lingo: "Hallelujah," "I'm blessed," "God is good all the time." But we haven't tasted Christ in a long time. The shadows are loud, but the presence is gone. And we don't even notice, because the shadows have replaced the substance.

Think of Peter at the Mount of Transfiguration. In Matthew 17:4, when he saw Jesus shining and Moses and Elijah beside Him, he said, "Lord, it is good for us to be here: if thou wilt, let us make here three tabernacles…" Peter was trying to turn a divine encounter into a permanent structure. He saw glory and immediately tried to make it a system. That's what we do when we are not careful. We experience God once, and instead of going deeper into Him, we build a system around that moment and stay there. Eventually, the system becomes our god. God never intended for shadows to become homes. They were meant to be signposts. The problem is that once we get a signpost, we stop traveling. But the signpost is not the city. The shadow is not the presence. The activity is not the intimacy. The fact that you are still around godly things does not mean you are growing.

This is how many of us find ourselves stuck in religious busyness while starving spiritually. We still quote scriptures, attend programs, and lead prayers. But if someone asks us, "When last did you feel God for real?" we look away in silence. Because shadows don't feed. Shadows only mimic. And yet, the scariest thing is how long we can survive off a shadow. We can build platforms, attract crowds, receive applause, gain followers, and engage in ministry, yet remain miles away from the Light. We do things for God, but no longer with God. And the tragedy is that nobody may notice, because the shadow still appears to be light. But deep inside, the True Light is missing.

Friend, this is not where you are supposed to stay. The shadows were never the destination. They were just a pathway, an introduction, an outline of something far greater: Jesus Christ, the True image, the full expression of God. Hebrews 1:3 describes Him as "the brightness of his glory, and the express image of his person..." Shadows fade. Images remain. Shadows point. Images stay. And if you want to stop wandering in the illusion, you must turn from the shadow to the Light, Jesus Christ. Because in the end, the only cure for shadow-chasing is to chase Christ.

TABLE OF CONTENTS

Chapter One

THE SUBTLE DRIFT

The devil knows that most people will not openly reject God. So, he simply adds things around them that take up their attention." - Rev. Dr. Nadine Nkulu

The Bible has always acknowledged the nature of the heart. Jeremiah 17:9 says, "The heart is deceitful above all things, and desperately wicked: who can know it?" That is not a statement made to discourage us, but to alert us. The very thing that we trust to lead us to fulfillment is also the part of us that can be easily misled. Because the heart has desires. And those desires, when not submitted to God, begin to look for other ways to be satisfied. It is still the same heart. But it starts to wander.

One of the earliest pictures of this truth is seen in Genesis 3. Eve was not initially looking to disobey God. She became interested in something she was told not to touch. When she saw that the tree was good for food and its fruit was pleasant to the eye, she took the fruit and ate. Eve's fall began with her eyes and a desire to get what she could not have. That is the first lie the devil tells many hearts today: that God has given you a good life, but something is missing, and that missing piece is what you must chase for satisfaction. This is the beginning of many journeys that look innocent. A man begins to work longer hours, not because his job does not pay well, but because he wants to provide more for his family. A young person begins to follow online voices, not to rebel against truth, but because online voices sound wise and give practical steps for self-improvement. A woman starts to pour her energy into raising children, not to discipline her kids, but to be a good mother. The heart is always searching. And when the searching is not properly guided, it becomes wandering. God designed the heart to be hungry so that it could find its satisfaction in Him. But the enemy takes advantage of that very hunger. He does not need to attack the heart with evil. He simply has to offer an alternative. It may look good, sound good, and even feel right. But if it takes the heart further from intimacy with God, then it is a shadow, not substance.

In Acts chapter 17, Paul stood in Athens and saw how deeply inquisitive people could be. In verse 22, he writes, "Ye men of Athens, I perceive that in all things ye are too superstitious." These were not lazy people. They were thinkers. Verse 21 says they spent their time either to tell or to hear something new. Paul respected their search, but he pointed out that they had missed the real answer. In verse 23, he said, "Whom therefore ye ignorantly worship, him declare I unto you." They had altars. They had conversations. But they were still wandering because God was unknown to them.

The modern believer can see themselves in that city. Many are searching for the One who gives meaning, but they do not realize that in all their searching, they have become distracted. The same mind that was meant to lead them to God has now built idols of success, reputation, affirmation, or independence.

Solomon understood this well. In Ecclesiastes, he went on a personal journey. He had wisdom, wealth, women, and influence. And yet, he wrote in Ecclesiastes 1:4, "I have seen all the works that are done under the sun; and, behold, all is vanity and vexation of spirit." Solomon was not a careless man. He was a man who chased after knowledge, comfort, and power. But even with all his gains, he confessed that nothing could satisfy the soul the way God could. This is where the danger lies. The devil knows that most people will not openly reject God. So, he adds things around them that take up their attention. Like he did with Eve, he highlights what they think they lack. Like he did with the Athenians, he surrounds them with endless alternatives. Like he did with Solomon, he offers them options that appear to lead to success but ultimately feel like emptiness.

In Matthew chapter 4, the devil tempted Jesus in the wilderness. In verse 3, he said, "If thou be the Son of God, command that these stones be made bread." The temptation was not about food alone. It was about proving identity through performance. Jesus responded in verse 4, "It is written, man shall not live by bread alone, but by every word that proceedeth out of the mouth of God." Jesus's response shows us something powerful. Man does not live by results. He lives by relationships. Fulfillment does not come from achievement, but from alignment.

Even the great prophet Elijah experienced this subtle wandering. In 1 Kings 19, after a powerful moment of calling down fire, he fled into the wilderness. He felt abandoned. He said in verse 10, "I have been very jealous for the LORD God of hosts: for the children of Israel have forsaken thy covenant... and I, even I only, am left." God later revealed Himself to Elijah, not in the wind or the fire, but in a still small voice. That voice reminded Elijah that intimacy with God is not found in external events but in quiet nearness.

A wandering heart may still be engaged in spiritual activities. It may still preach, sing, worship, volunteer, and even lead. But beneath the noise, it senses a gap. That gap grows when God becomes familiar instead of personal. When spiritual growth is measured by how much someone does, rather than how much they know God.

In Revelation 3, Jesus addressed the church in Laodicea. Verse 17 says, "Because thou sayest, I am rich, and increased with goods, and have need of nothing; and knowest not that thou art wretched, and miserable, and poor, and blind, and naked." That is what a wandering heart often looks like. It believes everything is fine, but it is unaware of how distant it has become. This is not always because of sin. Sometimes it is simply because the heart is wandering. It explores places that God disapproved of.

In Proverbs 14:12, it says, "There is a way which seemeth right unto a man, but the end thereof are the ways of death." This verse is not just for sinners. It is for the believer who thinks a path is good, useful, or beneficial, but it leads away from life. The enemy does not always have to turn the heart against God. He only needs to offer a path that seems better.

Paul warned Timothy in 2 Timothy 4:3, "For the time will come when they will not endure sound doctrine; but after their own lusts shall they heap to themselves teachers, having itching ears." Paul speaks of a generation that will follow voices that please their feelings, not their faith. That will chase after what sounds inspiring but does not deepen the connection with God. That is the heart that wanders.

So many believers today are exhausted. Not because they are lazy, but because they are chasing shadows. They attend everything, but they feel nothing. They serve everyone, but they are not satisfied. They quote promises, but they do not sense presence. They want more, but they still lack.

UNDERSTANDING HOW DISTANCE FROM GOD BEGINS

"The devil knows that the easiest way to distance a man from God is to influence a man's heart." - Rev. Dr. Nadine Nkulu

Jesus said in John 8:44 that the devil is not only a liar, but the father of lies. From the beginning, deception has been his weapon. In Genesis chapter 3, the story of the fall of man began with subtlety. In this chapter, the serpent is described as more subtle than any beast God had made. The serpent was not just a talking animal, but a voice of distortion and a master of twisted truth. He began deceiving Eve by asking a question that was designed to sow doubt. Yea, hath God said, "Ye shall not eat of every tree of the garden? This was not just a random question. It was a trap. A carefully laid scheme. A structure to weaken Eve's confidence in what God had clearly said. That is still the method the devil uses today. He will not ask man to walk away from God. He will suggest another option that seems equally meaningful. He will not tell men to deny the truth. He will ask him

4

to consider a different interpretation. The plan is to create distance. That is all he needs. A small space. A crack. A little gap. And that distance, when not noticed, begins to widen. Before man knows it, he has drifted away from where he used to be. He no longer feels the same fire. He no longer hears God as he used to. His discernment grows weak. He becomes busy, but empty. Engaged, but distracted. The soul has begun to move, even though the body is still in church.

The journey of distance begins when the heart starts to entertain thoughts that were once forbidden. It begins when compromise is no longer avoided but rationalized. In Proverbs chapter 4:23, the instruction is clear, "Keep thy heart with all diligence; for out of it are the issues of life." The word "keep" means to guard, to watch over. The reason is that the heart is the control center. The devil knows that if he can influence a man's heart, he has already begun the process of distancing man from God.

One of the most profound examples of this is in the life of Solomon. In 1 Kings 11:4, the scripture says, "For it came to pass, when Solomon was old, that his wives turned away his heart after other gods." It did not say they forced him. It said they turned away his heart. That shift did not happen overnight. It was gradual. It began with affection. It grew into tolerance. And then it became allegiance. Solomon, who once prayed with great wisdom and sought God with sincere devotion, eventually allowed his soul to drift. And the Bible records in verse 6 that, "Solomon did evil in the sight of the Lord, and went not fully after the Lord, as did David his father."

Distance from God always begins with not pursuing Him fully. It is not necessarily about running in the opposite direction. Sometimes, it is about slowing down. It is about becoming cold. Lukewarmness is a sign of drifting. In Revelation chapter 3:16, Jesus told the church in Laodicea, "So then because thou art lukewarm, and neither cold nor hot, I will spue thee out of my mouth." This was a group of believers who had works. They had gatherings. They had a form of spiritual life. But they had lost their passion. Their souls had started to distance themselves from God.

The truth is that the devil knows the power of proximity. He knows that as long as a man remains close to God, he is safe. He cannot do much to a soul that is wrapped in divine presence. That is why his strategy is not always destruction. Sometimes, it is distraction. It is the art of making the soul comfortable in activity without intimacy. A man can be busy for God and far from God. A man can speak in tongues and still not hear the voice of God clearly. This is how distance begins. It begins with a spiritual routine and the absence of spiritual reality.

In the book *Ordering Your Private World* by Gordon MacDonald, he wrote, "If my private world is in order, it will be because I am convinced that the inner world of the spiritual must govern the outer world of activity." The devil wants the outer world to govern. He wants man to measure closeness to God by success, crowds, busyness, and public achievements. But intimacy is not measured by the applause of people. It is measured by the posture of the soul before God.

There are times when man does not even know that he is drifting. He still prays. He still attends services. He still lifts his hands in worship. But something is missing. There is no more hunger. No more thirst. When the heart is no longer thirsty for God, the soul is already in motion. It is moving away slowly and quietly.

The enemy knows that once distance is established, the sensitivity of the soul drops. The convictions weaken. The clarity of purpose fades. And in that space of confusion, he introduces alternatives. Just like he did with Eve. The forbidden fruit was not presented as evil. It was presented as desirable.

Many believers today cannot trace when the shift began. They just woke up one day and noticed that their spiritual strength was not what it used to be. That is how distance works. It does not come with a loud announcement. It creeps in. It grows in silence. It expands in the absence of self-examination. That is why Paul said in 2 Corinthians 13:5, "Examine yourselves, whether ye be in the faith; prove your own selves."

Self-examination is not a religious exercise. It is a spiritual necessity. It is the only way to detect when the soul is beginning to drift. Without it, a man can continue doing good things and still end up far from God. This was the case with the prodigal son. His journey did not begin when he entered a far country. It began when he said to his father, "Father, give me the portion of goods that falleth to me" (Luke 15:12). That statement revealed a change of heart. A shift in focus. He still lived under the same roof at that point. But his soul had started to travel.

There are moments when distance begins, even as the body remains present. A husband can be in the house but emotionally disconnected from his wife. A person can be physically in the church but mentally absent. That is how it is with God. The devil is not trying to remove man from church. He is trying to remove God from his soul. He is trying to silence the inner voice. He is trying to replace conviction with convenience. To win this battle, man must understand the tactics of the enemy. He must learn to recognize the signs of spiritual distance.

SIGNS THAT YOU ARE MOVING AWAY WITHOUT KNOWING IT

"Intimacy is not about activity. It is not about volume or visibility. It is about union. It is about heart-to-heart connection. It is a deep, living awareness of God's presence." - Rev Dr. Nadine Nkulu

If a man knew he was drifting, he would most likely fight his way back. But the danger lies in not knowing, in being blind to the distance, in thinking that everything is fine simply because the external motions continue. But what is true intimacy? What does it really mean to be close to God? Not just in position, but in passion? Intimacy is not about activity. It is not about volume or visibility. It is about union. It is about heart-to-heart connection. It is a deep, living awareness of God's presence. It is the continuous longing to please God, hear Him, and walk with Him.

In Genesis 5:24, the Bible said, "Enoch walked faithfully with God; then he was no more, because God took him away." Enoch's walk with God was not casual. It was not a religious duty. It was a life of unbroken fellowship. The kind of intimacy that makes the physical realm too limited for one who has known such closeness. God took him. Because that relationship had become so real, so pure, so constant. The devil fears this kind of intimacy. He fears it because it is a place where deception cannot thrive.

Now, consider what happens when that intimacy begins to decline. The first sign is often invisible. It occurs in the secret places of the soul. A once-vibrant prayer life becomes routine. Worship becomes more about sound than spirit. The hunger for the Word fades, not immediately, but gradually. The man still attends church. He still quotes scripture. He still participates. But he no longer burns inside. The flame has weakened.

In Matthew 15:8, Jesus said, "These people honor me with their lips, but their hearts are far from me." That is the definition of drifting. When the lips are near, but the heart is far. It is a contradiction that religion permits but intimacy rejects. Intimacy demands the presence of the heart. Religion can function with the absence of heart, but not intimacy.

Another sign of drifting is found in the life of Samson. In Judges 16:20, after Delilah shaved off the seven locks of his head, she called, "Samson, the Philistines are upon you!" Samson awoke from his sleep and thought, 'I'll go out as before and shake myself free.' But he did not know that the Lord had left him." That last phrase is one of the most terrifying in scripture I have come to understand. "He did not know." He had no idea that the power had left. He still assumed that everything was intact. He did not know that his intimacy with God had already been broken.

This is how many believers live. They still function. They still perform. But the divine presence has shifted. The heart is no longer alive to God. Sensitivity is gone. Discernment is dulled. There is no more conviction when sin is near. No more sorrow over disobedience. Just a quiet resignation to spiritual emptiness.

When intimacy breaks, the signs are many. One of them is dryness in spiritual experience. Prayer becomes mechanical. The Word becomes boring. Fellowship feels like a duty. The spirit is no longer stirred. The soul is no longer moved. In Isaiah 29:13, God said, "These people come near to me with their mouth and honor me with their lips, but their hearts are far from me. Their worship of me is based on merely human rules they have been taught." The phrase "come near to me with their mouth" and "honor me with their lips" speaks to external acts—sacrifices, prayers, lip service—that do not reflect heartfelt commitment. The warning is that such hollow worship is meaningless in God's eyes.

Another sign is the shift from faith to form. The man no longer believes with his heart. He only repeats what he heard. There is no personal encounter. No fresh revelation. He depends on past experiences. He lives on borrowed light. In 2 Timothy 3:5, Paul described such people as having a form of godliness but denying the power thereof. The power is not in the words. It is in the presence. When that presence is gone, all that remains is a form.

Also, drifting manifests in disobedience that is no longer alarming. The conscience is no longer sharp. What was once considered wrong is now redefined. The man begins to negotiate obedience. He begins to explain away conviction. He no longer trembles at the Word. In Jeremiah 6:15, God said,

"Are they ashamed of their detestable conduct? No, they have no shame at all; they do not even know how to blush." It is dangerous when sin no longer stings. When error no longer provokes repentance.

Another sign is the replacement of divine instruction with personal ambition. When a man begins to pursue what he wants and puts God's will as an option, he has already drifted. He may still say the right things. But his heart is no longer submissive. He is no longer led. He is now leading himself. And that is a path that always ends in sorrow (Proverbs 14:12).

Now, how can a man know when the rope of his intimacy with God is breaking? How can he detect the weakening of his connection? The answer lies in awareness and in self-examination. In Psalm 139:23-24, David said, "Search me, God, and know my heart; test me and know my anxious thoughts. See if there is any offensive way in me, and lead me in the way everlasting." That is the prayer of a man who does not want to drift. That is the posture that keeps a soul close to God.

Another test is in the fruit. Jesus said in Matthew 7:20, "Thus, by their fruits we will recognize them." Intimacy with God always produces fruit. Love. Joy. Peace. Faithfulness. Gentleness. These are not random traits. They are proofs of union. When these begin to vanish, the rope is loosening. The vine is no longer supplying sap. The branches are drying up.

There is also a test in hunger. When a man no longer hungers for God, he has started to drift. Hunger is the first sign of life. In Matthew 5:6, Jesus said, "Blessed are they which do hunger and thirst after righteousness: for they shall be filled." No hunger, no filling. No thirst, no encounter. Hunger is a sign that the soul is still alive.

Another indication is in the way correction is received. A man who is drifting will resist correction. He will argue with truth. He will justify compromise. But intimacy teaches submission. It bows. It repents. It adjusts. Correction is not rejection. It is love in action. But the drifting soul sees it as an attack.

Drifting also shows in the way time is spent. The soul that is intimate with God makes time for Him. It does not rush devotion. It prioritizes communion. However, when intimacy is broken, other things begin to take over: entertainment, work, friends, noise. Everything becomes urgent. But the most essential thing is neglected. That is how the rope snaps, quietly, but gradually.

In the book *The Pursuit of God* by A. W. Tozer, he wrote, "The man who has God for his treasure has all things in One." That is the secret. God must be the treasure. Not the ministry. Not the gift. Not the platform. Just God. When that focus is lost, intimacy suffers.

DISCUSSION QUESTIONS

1. In a world full of endless entertainment, notifications, and opportunities, what subtle "good things" do you think most often steal believers' attention away from intimacy with God?

2. Eve was not looking for rebellion—she became distracted. What modern distractions do you think operate like the serpent's "pleasant fruit," looking harmless but slowly weakening spiritual focus?

3. Paul observed in Athens that people spent their time chasing something new. How does the modern hunger for new content, new ideas, or new voices affect the way Christians pursue truth today?

4. A wandering heart often remains active in spiritual routines. What are practical warning signs today that activity is replacing intimacy with God?

5. Solomon had everything yet felt empty. What are examples today of people achieving success but still feeling spiritually dissatisfied, and why do you think that happens?

6. Jesus resisted temptation by relying on God's Word rather than performance or results. How can we today reshape our identity so it is rooted in God, not in productivity, popularity, or external achievements?

7. Since drifting usually begins quietly, what habits of self-examination or accountability can help you recognize spiritual distance early—before it becomes a crisis?

Chapter Two

SHADOWS OF SUBSTITUTES

N othing from the devil is original. What he gives is a shadow,
a substitute." - Rev. Dr. Nadine Nkulu

Shadows are interesting things. They are not the real object.
They only show that the object is nearby. In science, a shadow is
formed when light shines on an object and that object blocks the
light, creating a dark shape that resembles the form of the object but
is not the object itself. That is what a shadow is in the natural sense.
It is an image, but not the image. It appears to be so, but it isn't. It
draws attention because it follows the object closely, but if someone
embraces the shadow instead of the real thing, then he has embraced
emptiness.

Let me show the psychological perspective of a shadow. In
psychology, shadows can represent hidden parts of a person's mind.
The part that one does not want others to see. The part that pretends,
that masks truth. In the journey of a man with God, shadows can

mean practices and activities that look like God but are not God. They seem spiritual. But they do not connect the soul with God.

In scripture, the word shadow was not used carelessly. It was used to describe temporary arrangements that pointed to something greater. The law was one of those arrangements. Paul the Apostle gave a sharp warning in Colossians 2:17. He spoke about certain holy days and religious observances and then said plainly, "Which are a shadow of things to come; but the body is of Christ." The law and the ceremonies that came with it were shadows. They pointed to something greater. They pointed to Christ.

Hebrews 10:1 gives an even more explicit statement. "For the law having a shadow of good things to come, and not the very image of the things, can never with those sacrifices which they offered year by year continually make the comers thereunto perfect."

The shadow had a purpose. It was not to be hated. It was to help men understand. But when the shadow begins to replace the real thing, the soul starts to drift into emptiness, believing itself to be full. That was what happened to many in the days of Jesus. The Pharisees were skilled at upholding the law, but they were blind to its true purpose. They had kept the shadow but rejected the substance. Christ said in John 5:39, "Search the scriptures; for in them ye think ye have eternal life: and they are they which testify of me." They had the scriptures. They had the shadow. But they missed the Person.

The devil is clever in his subtle operations. He never gives people things that obviously appear fake. Instead, he provides them imitations that carry traces of the original. He does not build a temple for idols and call it a distraction. No. He enters into what already exists and injects shadows. If God gives a prayer life, the devil presents a substitute. That substitute may still involve long hours of prayer, but it lacks intimacy. It may involve public displays, but it lacks power. If God gives love, the devil presents emotional attachments that look like care but are rooted in selfishness.

Many Christians today have a spiritual life centered on shadows. They are busy, but not burning with holy fire. They are active but not aligned. They are sincere, but they are sincerely missing the most important thing. A man can spend every morning reciting verses without ever hearing God. He can attend church services regularly without ever sitting in private prayer with God. He may cry during worship, but never change in his walk. These are not signs of rebellion. They are signs of substitution. A man has replaced presence with routine.

In the devil's workshop, there is no such thing as truth. He cannot create original things. He only builds lookalikes. He packages a form of godliness without power. That was why Paul warned in 2 Timothy 3:5 about having "a form of godliness, but denying the power thereof." It looks like God. It sounds like God. But God is not in it. The fire is not there. The connection is gone. But the activity remains. That is the painful thing about shadows. They stay even when the real object has moved.

Hebrews 8:5 also describes how the tabernacle built by Moses was only a copy of the true tabernacle. "Who serve unto the example and shadow of heavenly things." It was not the main tabernacle. It was a shadow. The devil took what was meant to guide people to truth and made it their final destination. The people became obsessed with the temple, the altar, and the rituals. They were clinging to the shadow while the real God stood among them in human form, and they could not recognize Him. Our world is not the first to experience this substitution.

The Bible gives us powerful examples of how people have turned God-given tools, symbols, and prophetic instruments into idols, worshiping the shadow instead of the substance. This illustrates a common human error: the failure to transition from a prophetic sign to the Person the sign pointed to.

THE BRONZE SERPENT: A SHADOW OF CHRIST THAT BECAME AN IDOL

God commanded Moses to make the bronze serpent when the children of Israel were bitten by serpents in the wilderness, "And the Lord said unto Moses, Make thee a fiery serpent, and set it upon a pole: and it shall come to pass, that every one that is bitten, when he looketh upon it, shall live." Numbers 21:8. This serpent on a pole was a God-ordained tool to bring healing. It was not meant to be worshiped; it was just a shadow pointing to something greater. Jesus later revealed what the bronze serpent really symbolized: "And as Moses lifted up the serpent in the wilderness, even so must the Son of man be lifted up: That whosoever believeth in him should not perish, but have eternal life." John 3:14-15

The serpent was a type of Christ on the cross, lifted up for healing and eternal life. The serpent was not the savior; it pointed to the Savior. But later, Israel turned that bronze serpent into an idol. Hundreds of years later, they were burning incense to it, worshiping it as if it had power, but Hezekiah destroyed it, calling it "Nehushtan" (meaning "a mere piece of brass"). What was once a prophetic tool became a snare because they idolized the shadow and forgot the God who gave it.

THE TEMPLE: A PLACE FOR GOD'S PRESENCE THAT BECAME A SYMBOL OF PRIDE

The temple was God's dwelling place."And let them make me a sanctuary; that I may dwell among them" Exodus 25:8. The Tabernacle, and later the Temple, was God's dwelling place on earth. But it was a shadow of a greater, heavenly reality. The temple was never to be trusted as a substitute for obedience. "Trust ye not in lying words, saying, The temple of the Lord, The temple of the Lord, The temple of the Lord, are these." Jeremiah 7:4

They assumed God's presence guaranteed safety just because the Temple was in their midst.

But God said, "Don't idolize the temple; it's obedience I want."

Jesus replaced the physical temple with his own body, "Jesus answered and said unto them, Destroy this temple, and in three days I will raise it up… But he spoke of the temple of his body." John 2:19, 21. Jesus pointed them away from the structure to the Person. The temple was a shadow of Christ's body. They idolized the building but rejected the Lord of the temple when He came.

THE ARK OF THE COVENANT: GOD'S PRESENCE MADE INTO A LUCKY CHARM

The ark was a symbol of god's presence.

"And there I will meet with thee, and I will commune with thee from above the mercy seat." Exodus 25:22. The Ark was a holy object, where God would speak to Moses, but Israel turned the ark into a magical object in battle. "And when the ark of the covenant of the Lord came into the camp, all Israel shouted with a great shout... the Philistines fought, and Israel was smitten... and the ark of God was taken."1 Samuel 4:5-11. The Israelites thought carrying the ark into battle guaranteed victory. But they idolized the object and forgot the God of the ark and were defeated. The ark was a tool for communion, not a magic box. Idolatry led to its capture.

God often uses symbols, signs, and prophetic tools to point us to Christ, but the danger is when we cling to the tool and forget the Teacher.

The Bible says, "Looking unto Jesus the author and finisher of our faith..." Hebrews 12:2 This is the code to real intimacy with God. It is built on Christ, not things and activities. When the devil wants to damage a believer, he does not always use sin. Sometimes, he uses something that looks good. Something that feels spiritual. Something that fits the religious framework. He gives substitutes. A counterfeit peace that comes from achievements instead of surrender. A counterfeit joy that comes from people's praises instead of God's presence. These things are shadows. They have a form. But they have no depth.

A young believer may start on fire, truly burning for God. But then life comes. Responsibilities grow. Distractions increase. Slowly, he begins to embrace the shadow. He no longer waits for God to speak. He repeats what others have said. He no longer weeps before God. He rehearses the motions. That is the subtle power of the substitute. It offers a more straightforward pathway. A pattern that does not demand brokenness. A practice that avoids pain. But it also avoids power.

In one of the great spiritual classics, *The Pursuit of God* by A. W. Tozer, he wrote, "It is not what a man does that determines whether his work is sacred or secular, it is why he does it." The heart behind the action determines whether it is a shadow or the real thing. Many today are chasing substitutes with clean motives but unaware hearts. The substitute cannot heal the soul. It cannot fill the void. It can only occupy space. And that is what the devil wants.

Substitutes do not come as temptations. They come as alternatives. They do not warn. They imitate. They do not destroy immediately. They drift. And when a man begins to drift in the spirit, he still thinks he is on course. He does not know that the substance is gone, and he is hugging the shadow.

God has not changed. He still seeks those who will worship in spirit and in truth. But the devil knows this, and so he feeds many believers with the shadows of truth. Things that resemble spirit. Actions that resemble worship. Words that resemble faith. But none of these has weight. They do not make the soul tremble. They do not make the man cry in the secret place. They are empty routines dressed as sacred experiences.

REPLACING GOD WITH GOOD THINGS

"The gold of communion cannot be traded for the brass of activity. If it is not God, then no matter how beautiful it looks, it is still a substitute." - Rev Dr. Nadine Nkulu

The story of Jeroboam comes to my mind as one of the earliest dangers of substitution in the kingdom. Jeroboam, after God handed the ten tribes of Israel into his hands, feared that if the people continued to go to Jerusalem to worship, their hearts would return to Rehoboam, the king of Judah. So, in 1 Kings 12:28, the Bible records, "Whereupon the king took counsel, and made two calves of gold, and said unto them, It is too much for you to go up to Jerusalem: behold thy gods, O Israel, which brought thee up out of the land of Egypt." That was a good idea from a human viewpoint. He was trying to preserve his kingdom and create an alternative that seemed safe. But in doing so, he crafted an image and called it god. That was not a rejection of worship but a redirection of it. A golden calf took the place of the living God.

There is a mystery in Exodus 32, where Aaron shaped a golden calf from the earrings of the people. The intention of the people was not to destroy themselves. They simply said in verse 1, "Up, make us gods, which shall go before us." They did not say, "Make us Satan." They wanted something to represent what Moses had represented. The idea was not evil in its packaging, but it became evil in its impact. The golden calf symbolized a positive thing to them because it offered visible leadership and presence. But in the realm of the spirit, it was rebellion. They danced, they sang, they worshiped, and they called it a feast to the Lord in verse 5. That is the danger of replacing God with good things. The form remains, but the presence is absent.

Let us examine a deeper concept using the case of Solomon. God blessed Solomon with wisdom and wealth. But in 1 Kings 11:4, the Bible says, "For it came to pass, when Solomon was old, that his wives turned away his heart after other gods: and his heart was not perfect with the Lord his God." Solomon did not lose God by a sudden rebellion. He was still building. He was still seated on the throne. He was still known as the wise king. Yet his heart had shifted. He did not run after evil in the beginning. He loved women. It is not a sin to love, but when that love becomes a doorway through which God is replaced in the soul, it becomes idolatry. His passion for women was good in the eyes of men, but it drew him away from the commandment of God. That which was permitted became the channel for disconnection. The substitute came in the form of affection.

Apostle Paul in Romans 1:25 says, "Who changed the truth of God into a lie, and worshipped and served the creature more than the Creator, who is blessed for ever." That is another way to say that men took good things and made them gods. They took creation and made it an idol. They admired the created so much that they forgot the Creator. A man may find himself so consumed with ministry that he forgets the God of the ministry. He may be buried in serving people so much that his personal walk with the Lord suffers. The doing replaces the being. The service replaces the intimacy. These things are not evil. But when the energy we are to use in knowing God is spent in doing things for God, even those things become shadows.

There is a remarkable example in 2 Chronicles 12:9-10. The Bible says, "So Shishak king of Egypt came up against Jerusalem, and took away the treasures of the house of the Lord, and the treasures of the king's house; he took all: he carried away also the shields of gold which Solomon had made. Instead of which king Rehoboam made shields of brass."

Gold was taken, but rather than seek the restoration of what was lost, brass was created to keep the image alive. Brass appears to be gold from a distance, but it is not gold. This is a powerful prophetic image of how substitutes enter our walk with God. When the golden intimacy is lost, men do not cry for restoration; they settle for routines. When fresh fire is gone, they do not wait for it to return; they settle for noise. When real prayer becomes hard, they echo words that do not reach the heavens. Brass is noisy. It makes a sound when struck, but it has no weight.

In Tozer's book *The Pursuit of God*, he wrote, "The tragedy is that our eternal welfare depends upon our hearing, and we have trained our ears not to hear." Many have traded the voice of God for the sound of activity. They have replaced the original hunger with comfort. That was never how it was meant to be. In the beginning, God walked with Adam in the cool of the day. That was the original design. That was true fulfillment. God was not seeking results from Adam. He was seeking relationship.

When Jesus visited Martha and Mary in Luke 10:38-42, Martha received Him into her house and became cumbered with much serving. Mary, however, sat at His feet. Jesus told Martha in verse 42, "But one thing is needful: and Mary hath chosen that good part, which shall not be taken away from her." Martha was doing something good, yet it was not the most important thing. This shows us that good things are not always the right things. That which is good may not be the will of God. The soul must be trained to discern between what looks good and what is truly God.

The devil often presents substitutes because he knows the heart of man is designed to worship. If he cannot make man sin, he will make him busy. If he cannot trap him in darkness, he will cloak him with light that is not from heaven. He will push men into celebrating works instead of presence. Men will then measure their standing with God based on the quantity of what they do, not the quality of their connection. This is why Jesus said in Matthew 7:22-23,

"Many will say to me in that day, Lord, Lord, have we not prophesied in thy name and in thy name have cast out devils and in thy name done many wonderful works? And then will I profess unto them, I never knew you: depart from me." They did good things. But they were strangers to the Master. They did not know Him. The replacement of God with good things can also be seen in Saul's attempt to offer a sacrifice. In 1 Samuel 13, when Samuel delayed, Saul offered the burnt offering. It was a good intention. He did not want the people to scatter. But it was not his place. Samuel said in verse 13, "Thou hast done foolishly: thou hast not kept the commandment of the Lord thy God." That was the beginning of his fall. Good things done in disobedience become rebellion. They look noble. They look sincere. But they are not approved.

People may pour themselves into giving, working, building, or even studying, and yet be far from God. When the goal of those things is no longer Him but the thing itself, then a substitute has taken root. There are men who have replaced the presence of God with knowledge about God. The knowledge becomes the idol. They speak of Him but do not know Him. Their lips are full, but their hearts are empty.

There is a call in this generation to return to what truly matters. The issue is not whether something is good. The question is whether it still allows room for intimacy. What men call progress may be the shadow of a more profound disconnection. What they call passion may be the mask of inner emptiness. The test is this: does it bring a man closer to God or take him further? Does it carry the weight of divine approval, or is it simply a noise of brass?

As believers, the question we must ask is not only what we do but why we do it. Not only what we pursue, but whether that pursuit still leaves room for God. The gold of communion cannot be traded for the brass of activity. If it is not God, then no matter how beautiful it looks, it is still a substitute. And a substitute, no matter how polished, can never satisfy the soul created for God.

WHEN RELIGION REPLACES RELATIONSHIP

"False religion measures people by their actions. True relationship transforms people through their encounters. In the end, what matters most is not how much was done but how close one walked."

The first thing to understand is that religion, by itself, is not inherently evil. The Bible does not condemn pure religion. James said, "Pure religion and undefiled before God and the Father is this, To visit the fatherless and widows in their affliction, and to keep himself unspotted from the world"(James 1:27). That is not empty ceremony. That is not lifeless tradition. That is service born out of love. That is action flowing from a relationship with the Father. However, when what man calls religion begins to stand as a replacement for a heart connection with God, it has lost its purpose and has begun to oppose the very thing it was meant to foster.

A careful study of Scripture shows that religion, in its corrupted form, became a major stumbling block to the people of Israel. In Isaiah chapter 1:1-15, God rejected their sacrifices, their incense, their new moons, and their appointed feasts. Why would God reject the very things He had once commanded? Because their hearts had departed from Him. The external observance continued, but the inner devotion had died. He told them to wash, make clean, put away the evil of their doings, and seek judgment. It was not their sacrifices that were the problem, but that those sacrifices had become a cover for a lack of relationship.

Jesus Himself confronted this issue face-to-face during His earthly ministry. In Matthew chapter 23, He addressed the scribes and Pharisees with some of the harshest words ever recorded from His lips. He called them hypocrites because they paid tithe of mint, anise, and cumin, but had omitted the weightier matters of the law, judgment, mercy, and faith. That is Matthew 23:23. They were experts in religious detail but strangers to the heart of God. He said, "These ought ye to have done, and not to leave the other undone."

In other words, their works were not wrong in themselves, but they had replaced the foundation, the relationship with the Father, with outward observance.

If salvation is not by works, then spiritual growth is not by works either. It is by grace. Paul made this clear in Galatians 3:3,

"Are ye so foolish? Having begun in the Spirit, are ye now made perfect by the flesh?"

Spiritual growth is not mechanical. It is not a ladder we climb by human effort. It is not a performance to be rated. It is a deepening relationship with a living God. Philippians chapter 2 verse 12 says,

"Work out your own salvation with fear and trembling."

But verse 13 says,

"For it is God which worketh in you both to will and to do of his good pleasure."

We do not produce the life. God works it in, and we work it out.

False religion is the devil's tool to wear out saints. It adds burdens God did not give. It multiplies rules and expectations that choke the life out of spiritual experience. Jesus warned in Matthew chapter 15, verse 9,

"But in vain they do worship me, teaching for doctrines the commandments of men."

That is the essence of religion without relationship. Worship becomes vain. Words become empty. Actions become hollow. Religion becomes a noise without life.

There are stories in the Bible that reveal the danger of replacing relationship with religion. One striking example is in Revelation 2:2-5, where Jesus commended the church in Ephesus for their works, their labor, their patience, and their hatred of evil. Yet He said,

"Nevertheless, I have somewhat against thee, because thou hast left thy first love."

The danger was not a lack of service, but the loss of intimacy. He told them to remember from where they had fallen and repent. That word repent was not for sin in the usual sense. It was for losing heart connection.

There are unconscious mindsets and activities that can gradually become ingrained as a religion. People can be involved in worship, prayer meetings, fasting, and other spiritual disciplines, and yet be far from God in their hearts. The motions can remain long after the emotion is gone. One can learn the language of religion, the vocabulary of prayer, and the expressions of worship, yet still be operating from memory rather than from a genuine connection. It is a slow fade, a gradual decline. And often, it is unnoticed until it is far gone.

One way to detect the shift is to ask what is feeding the soul. Is it God's presence, or is it applause? Is it communion with God, or is it routine? Is prayer a lifeline or a checklist? Does worship move the heart or just fill the schedule? These are not condemning questions. They are diagnostic. The goal is not guilt. It is return.

Another way to test the health of one's relationship with God is to observe how one responds when there is no audience. Relationship with God thrives in the secret place. Religion survives on visibility. When a person can sit with God in silence, when there is no platform, no microphone, no recognition, and still find satisfaction, then that person is walking in relationship. But when activity is needed to feel close to God, there is a risk of replacing connection with motion.

The Bible warns against a form of godliness that denies the power thereof. That is Second Timothy chapter 3:5. A form of godliness is religion. The power is relationship. Without the Spirit, religion is lifeless. Without love, religion is noise. First Corinthians 13:1 says,

"Though I speak with the tongues of men and of angels, and have not charity, I am become as sounding brass or a tinkling cymbal."

That is what happens when religion replaces relationship.

Jesus said in John chapter 15:5,

"Without me ye can do nothing."

That was not a poetic statement. It was a spiritual reality. He is the vine. We are the branches. Apart from Him, there is no life. The moment a person starts to function apart from intimacy with Him, they are already disconnected. The fruit may remain for a while, but the withering is inevitable.

One of the most subtle dangers is that religion can look like spiritual maturity. People may admire consistency, discipline, dedication, and service. But only God sees the heart. That is why David prayed in Psalm 139:23,

"Search me, O God, and know my heart: try me, and know my thoughts."

He knew that even a man after God's heart could drift.

True relationship is not marked by perfection but by connection. It is about being real with God. It is about walking with Him daily, talking with Him honestly, listening to His voice, and responding in love. It is not about performance. It is about presence.

False religion measures people by their actions. True relationship transforms people through their encounters. In Acts chapter 4:13, the boldness of Peter and John was noted, and it was said they had been with Jesus. That is the fruit of relationship.

In the end, what matters most is not how much was done but how close one walked. Jesus warned in Matthew chapter 7:22-23,

"Many will say to me in that day, Lord, Lord, have we not prophesied in thy name? And in thy name have cast out devils? And in thy name done many wonderful works? And then will I profess unto them, I never knew you. Depart from me."

That is the ultimate picture of religion without relationship—many works. No connection.

The call of this chapter is to return. Return to simplicity. Return to first love. Return to the place where God's presence is more than enough. It is not a call to abandon action but to align action with affection. It is not a rejection of discipline but a reminder that discipline is a means, not an end. Everything we do should flow from love for God.

This is the heart of fulfillment. When man lives in communion with his Maker, when activity flows from intimacy, and when actions are birthed from relationship, then religion becomes alive, and life becomes full. It is not a matter of doing more. It is a matter of abiding more. As Jesus said in John chapter 15:7,

"If ye abide in me, and my words abide in you, ye shall ask what ye will, and it shall be done unto you."

DISCUSSION QUESTIONS

1. What modern "good things" (e.g. success, ministry, family, self-care, online influence, productivity) are most likely to become substitutes for intimacy with God, and how can you recognize when this shift is happening in your life?

2. Many Christians today live busy, impressive spiritual lives outwardly but feel empty inwardly. What are some practical signs that a person is operating in a form of godliness without the power of genuine relationship with God?

3. One can pray, worship, and serve, yet disconnected from God. How can you intentionally rebuild a lifestyle where your private devotion to God matters more than public activity?

4. If the devil cannot make a believer fall into obvious sin, he often gives them a polished substitute. What are common spiritual substitutes today that appear holy but actually push a person away from God?

5. Shadows are convincing because they resemble the real thing. What habits or spiritual practices can help you continually test whether what you are holding onto is God or only a shadow shaped like God?

Chapter Three

THE NOISE BETWEEN YOU AND GOD

The noise between you and God is yours to stop. Noise is not just an unwanted sound; it is also a connection breaker."
- Rev. Dr. Nadine Nkulu

The experience Kenneth Hagin shared in *I Believe in Visions* makes the concept of noise clear. In the vision, he was speaking with Jesus Christ face-to-face. Then, a monkeylike demon appeared, jumping between them, pouring dark smoke, and making distracting noise. The communication became unclear. Jesus kept talking, but Kenneth could no longer hear. He wondered why Jesus did not do something about the disruption until he realized it was his responsibility to rebuke the demon. Once he did, the noise disappeared. The lesson there is deep. God can still be present and still be speaking, yet a believer may hear nothing because of the noise in between. And unless one takes responsibility to silence the interference, the conversation breaks down.

Biblically, noise is not simply sound waves or distractions. It is anything that challenges the clarity of divine communication. One example is found in Job 33. Elihu, the younger man among Job's friends, offered a perspective that many of his friends overlooked. He said, "For God speaketh once, yea twice, yet man perceiveth it not" (Job 33:14).

That is what noise does. It causes a person to miss what was already spoken. God speaks, not once, but multiple times. But when there is internal or external interference, the message gets lost. Perception becomes clouded.

There are moments when the human heart becomes too full to hear God. In Ezekiel 14:3, the elders of Israel came to inquire of the Lord, but God said,

"These men have set up their idols in their heart, and put the stumbling block of their iniquity before their face: should I be enquired of at all by them?"

These idols were not carved images. They were internal fixations, things they loved more than truth. These inner attachments created spiritual static. Though they wanted to hear God, the noise within them became louder than their sincerity. Their hearts had already chosen what they wanted to hear, so the real voice of God became unbearable to them.

Noise breaks relationships in the same way silence does: by filling the space with assumptions. When someone does not hear God clearly, they begin to create their own interpretations of what they believe. That is how golden calves are built in the modern day, not always with gold, but with goals. People begin to chase what sounds spiritual but lacks the breath of God. In Amos 8:11, the Lord warned of a famine, not of bread or water, but of hearing the words of the Lord. That verse is haunting. Not a famine of God's voice, but of the ability to hear it. When noise becomes a lifestyle, even hunger for truth becomes empty.

Imagine walking through a busy marketplace trying to take a phone call. The person on the other end is speaking, but the environment is chaotic. If you are not intentional, you may hang up. Not because the person stopped speaking, but because you can no longer hear them. That is what happens spiritually. People hang up on God without realizing it. They lose interest. They grow impatient. They assume He is silent. But He was never quiet. They just stopped listening.

Noise is also layered. It is not always external. Sometimes it is the memory of a past hurt, the echo of disappointment, the craving for success, or the pressure to be approved. These inner sounds form what psychologists might call mental chatter, but in spiritual terms, they are considered interference. These thoughts move in circles and eventually build an altar. When God tries to speak, the heart is already occupied. Jeremiah 6:10 shows us a painful image:

"To whom shall I speak, and give warning, that they may hear? Behold, their ear is uncircumcised, and they cannot hearken."

God spoke, but the people's ears were not prepared. That is what noise does; it makes the soul unready.

There is a concept we must take seriously: getting lost in the noise. To be lost in noise is to enter a journey with no map, only motion. It is movement without destination. It is when a person follows everything that sounds urgent and ends up arriving at nothing that brings peace. This is why Isaiah 30:15 remains powerful:

"In returning and rest shall ye be saved; in quietness and in confidence shall be your strength: and ye would not."

The people refused quietness. They rejected stillness. And so, they remained vulnerable. Lost in the noise.

Sometimes the noise between God and man is caused by expectations. People expect God to speak a certain way, or to speak when they want Him to, or to confirm what they have already decided. And when He does not do that, they fill the gap with other voices. Jeremiah 23:16 captures this reality:

"Hearken not unto the words of the prophets that prophesy unto you: they make you vain: they speak a vision of their own heart, and not out of the mouth of the Lord."

Here, God exposed the kind of noise that pretends to be prophecy. The noise that wears the clothing of spirituality but carries no truth. This is how the devil has successfully distracted many, by letting the noise look holy.

There is also the noise of busyness. Not sinful busyness. Just unending activity. Ecclesiastes 5:1 warns,

"Keep thy foot when thou goest to the house of God, and be more ready to hear, than to give the sacrifice of fools."

Sometimes people rush into God's presence with offerings, declarations, and performance, but never stop to listen. The noise of doing replaces the silence of being. So even in church, the heart becomes disconnected.

Noise, if left unchecked, becomes a pattern. It conditions the soul to respond to pressure instead of presence. And when someone lives this way long enough, they become strangers to the still voice of God. Think of Samuel as a child in the temple. God called him multiple times, but he assumed it was Eli. The voice of God sounded too familiar. It was not until Eli recognized what was happening that Samuel knew how to respond. The noise was not evil. It was simply a matter of inexperience in discernment. And that is another danger. Sometimes the noise is ignorance—the inability to tell who is speaking.

THE TYRANNY OF BUSYNESS

"The devil does not always have to take a person back to sin; he just needs to make them too busy for intimacy with God."

The enemy has studied patterns and knows the human heart well. He knows that people cry to God for blessings, and when they receive them, they tend to forget the Giver. A person who once knelt in prayer for a child may eventually get so caught up with the child that they no longer kneel. One who cried for a spouse may end up using that marriage as a reason for spiritual distance. What began as an answered prayer becomes an excuse. The devil does not always have to take a person back to sin; he just needs to make them too busy to pray.

Let us take, for example, a man who was unemployed for years. During that time, he attended prayer meetings faithfully. He fasted often. He volunteered. He stayed in the presence of God. Then came the job. A great job. Answered prayer. But now his schedule is full. Meetings. Deadlines. Clients. He still loves God, but he no longer has time. That man is now under the tyranny of busyness. He is busy but slowly drifting.

In Luke 14:18-20, Jesus told a parable of those who were invited to a great supper. One said he had bought a piece of land and needed to go see it. Another said he bought five yokes of oxen. Another said he had married a wife. All these people had genuine reasons. None of them was doing anything sinful. But they all missed the invitation. Busyness won.

When blessings become burdens, the soul begins to die quietly. Nobody notices it at first because everything still appears to be in order on the outside. They still post Scriptures. They still attend events. But the fire is gone. The time that once belonged to God has been divided. It is not that they chose evil; they just let life take over. And that is how many have fallen, while succeeding.

The devil is smart enough to use organization to enforce this pattern. There are work systems that have been carefully designed to remove rest, silence, and spiritual reflection. How can a person work from Sunday to Saturday, seven in the morning till seven in the evening? How do they nurture their soul? How do they sit still before God? The world claps for them. The company gives them awards. But heaven knows they are enslaved.

When Pharaoh enslaved the children of Israel in Egypt, he did not do it by killing them. He made them busy. When Moses came to demand their release, Pharaoh increased their workload. In Exodus 5:9, Pharaoh said,

"Let there more work be laid upon the men, that they may labour therein; and let them not regard vain words."

His goal was clear: keep them so busy they would not have time to listen to truth. That strategy is still working today. Many cannot even consider what God is saying because their schedules are already choking them.

There is also the subtle trap of being busy with what God gave. Imagine a man who received a vision from God. He builds the vision, expands the assignment, and gathers a team. Slowly, the work becomes bigger than the relationship. He begins to study for sermons but not to know God. He leads prayers but does not pray.

He mentors others but neglects his own altar. The assignment now stands where intimacy once stood. God gave it, but now it has taken God's place. That man is not backslidden, but he is empty.

Some busy people carry guilt silently. They want to slow down, but they feel obligated to keep moving. They remember how they used to pray, how they used to wait, how they used to be available. But now they are trapped. The same world that praised their commitment now holds them hostage. They do not know how to return without appearing to be failures. That is the quiet pain of spiritual busyness. It does not give peace. It only gives results that do not satisfy.

There are biblical figures who got busy and missed out. Saul, for example, was chosen by God. But when God sent him to destroy Amalek, he got busy with preserving what God said to destroy. In 1 Samuel 15:17, Samuel said,

"When thou wast little in thine own sight, wast thou not made the head of the tribes of Israel?"

Saul had started well. But success made him self-reliant. Busyness led him to disobedience. Eventually, he lost the throne.

Another example is Solomon. He loved the Lord at the beginning. He prayed with tears. He built the temple. But in 1 Kings 11, he began to marry foreign wives and build altars for their gods. He became busy maintaining the peace of his empire. He gave room for other worship to please his partners. Slowly, his heart turned. God did not change. Solomon did. He got so engaged in management that he lost his walk.

Busyness is not just physical movement. It is mental occupation. A person can be lying in bed but unable to rest. Their minds are running through tasks, calls, debts, and plans. The soul becomes noisy. And when they try to pray, they feel a sense of dryness. The altar becomes a duty, not a delight. That is not just a distraction. That is bondage.

In some cases, even the church contributes to this. A believer can become overwhelmed with activities, such as rehearsals, meetings, programs, and projects, leaving little time for quiet devotion. They become efficient servants but disconnected sons. The ministry moves forward, but their heart stays behind. They are applauded for performance, but heaven is silent.

When Jesus walked the earth, He often withdrew from the crowds. In Mark 1:35, He rose early in the morning to pray in a solitary place. In Luke 5:16, He withdrew into the wilderness. Even the Son of God did not let busyness own Him. He chose solitude intentionally. That was not weakness. That was wisdom.

There are moments when a person must choose between success and stillness. The world will always push for more. But heaven still waits for less. Less noise. Less movement. Less ambition. And more awareness. Awareness of God's presence. Awareness of His leading. Awareness of His heart.

A quote from Watchman Nee says, "Busyness often substitutes for a lack of faith. We believe that if we do not take action, nothing will happen. But God often waits until we are still before He moves." This is not poetic. It is a principle. The Spirit of God moves most clearly in stillness. Not in the storm. Not in the fire. But in the small, quiet whisper.

The real danger of the tyranny of busyness is that it does not kill the body. It just slowly drains the soul like a leaking bucket. A person may not feel the loss immediately. But over time, they wake up and realize they are far from where they started. Their fire has become ashes. Some are so used to being busy that silence makes them nervous. They do not know how to sit before God for more than five minutes without checking the clock. They pray while checking messages. They study while replying to emails. They sing while worrying about the next meeting. Their minds are never present. And because of this, they leave every spiritual moment half-fed.

HOW DISTRACTIONS STEAL INTIMACY

"Distraction is the slow death of spiritual fire. It happens like leakage. Every little thing pulls a drop of passion until the vessel is empty." - Rev Dr. Nadine Nkulu

In the Book of Judges, there was a man named Samson. He was not an ordinary man. He carried divine strength and an explicit instruction. No razor was to touch his head. No compromise was to enter his heart. He was born for deliverance. But he was distracted. His eyes began to wander. His heart followed his eyes. He moved from one woman to another until he met Delilah. What Delilah could not do with power, she did with persistence. She did not fight him. She distracted him. Over time, the distraction stole his focus. Then his hair was cut, and his strength was gone. Not in one day. But slowly. That is how distraction works. It removes intimacy drop by drop.

David was a man after God's own heart. He was a worshiper, a warrior, a king. But in 2 Samuel 11, he stayed back when kings were supposed to go to war. He stepped out onto his roof and saw a woman bathing. The moment he fixed his eyes, his focus shifted. He forgot the battles he had won. He forgot the songs he had written. That distraction led him to adultery, then murder, and eventually spiritual silence. For a season, David was no longer the man on the hill singing to God. He was now a man hiding from God. That is the power of distraction. It does not just change your action. It distances your affection.

One of the clearest examples in the New Testament is found in Matthew 14. Peter saw Jesus walking on the sea and asked to come. Jesus said, "Come." And Peter walked on water. It was real. He walked until he saw the wind. That moment of attention shift cost him balance. He sank. What changed was not the sea. What changed was focus. That is how distraction works. It shifts the eyes, then shakes the soul. Intimacy cannot survive when the eyes are everywhere.

Many believers underestimate the danger of divided attention. They think that as long as they still believe in God, they are safe. But intimacy does not survive on belief alone. It survives on focus. A husband and wife may still be married, but if they stop looking into each other's lives, the warmth dies. That is how it is with God. He does not move. He does not change. But distraction steals the gaze.

In Luke 8:14, Jesus explained the parable of the sower. He said,

"And that which fell among thorns are they, which, when they have heard, go forth, and are choked with cares and riches and pleasures of this life, and bring no fruit to perfection."

That is distraction. It is not always sin. Sometimes it is just care. Just pleasure. Just the need to survive. These things grow like thorns and wrap around the soul until nothing can grow anymore. The seed of intimacy dies not because of evil, but because of everything else.

Some people once had deep wells of prayer. They used to sit in silence and hear God. They used to wake up hungry for the Word. Now their phones wake them up. Their schedules drive them. Their minds are filled with everything except the presence. They still love God, but they are no longer close. Distraction has replaced desire. And the worst part is that it looks normal. Everyone else is the same. Everyone is busy. Everyone is moving. So, they do not see it as a problem. But something is gone. Something holy. Something deep.

Distraction is the slow death of spiritual fire. It does not happen like a crash. It happens like a leak. Every little thing pulls a drop of passion until the vessel is empty. The person still serves. Still gives. Still attends. But the eyes are dry. The altar is cold. God becomes an idea, not a reality. That is what happened to the church in Revelation 2.

Jesus said, "Nevertheless I have somewhat against thee, because thou hast left thy first love."

They were still there. Still active. But something was missing. Intimacy.

The enemy does not need to remove a person from church. He only needs to remove their heart from God. Distraction is a silent weapon. It keeps the body in motion but the soul in absence. The man who used to sit at the feet of Jesus is now running around for the world. The woman who once wept in worship is now rushing through her devotions. Not because they turned away. But because they got distracted.

A quote from A.W. Tozer says, "The world is perishing for lack of the knowledge of God, and the Church is famishing for want of His presence." Distraction does not just affect the individual; it also weakens those around them. It weakens the whole Body. When intimacy is lost, direction is lost. When direction is lost, purpose is delayed. Distraction is not about losing moments. It is about losing seasons.

Some people do not even notice they have changed. Their

language is still the same. Their routines have not shifted. But their hunger is gone. Their tears are gone. Their worship has become a performance. Their study has become a task. That is what happens when the heart is no longer fixed. In Psalm 57:7, David said,

"My heart is fixed, O God, my heart is fixed: I will sing and give praise."

That kind of heart is not common. It must be trained. It must be guarded because everything in this world wants to distract.

Even spiritual things can become a distraction. Ministry can become a distraction. Success can become a distraction. Family can become a distraction. When anything takes the place of attention, it becomes a thief of our focus. The thief does not always break in with violence. Sometimes, he enters with kindness. That is why Paul warned in 1 Corinthians 7:35 that even in marriage, one must serve the Lord without distraction.

A distracted person becomes weak over time. Not because they have sinned, but because they have lost awareness. Their eyes are no longer on the beauty of the Lord. Their ears are no longer tuned to His heartbeat. They live, but they do not feel. They move, but they do not grow. They perform, but they do not transform. That is what it means to be lost in the shadows.

DISCUSSION QUESTIONS

1. Many people assume God is silent when life feels chaotic. How can a believer tell the difference between God's silence and simply being too noisy internally to hear Him?

2. How does busyness today (work deadlines, family responsibilities, endless to-do lists) can subtly become a spiritual enemy, even when everything on the schedule is good?

3. Social media creates constant comparison and pressure. How might this modern mental chatter become the kind of 'noise' that clouds a believer's perception of God's direction?

4. When does spiritual activity- serving, volunteering, attending events can become its own form of noise, keeping people busy for God but disconnected from God?

5. What practices can someone adopt to recognize early signs that they are "lost in the noise"—that their soul is moving constantly but arriving nowhere spiritually?

6. In a world that values speed, results, and productivity, how can believers reclaim the discipline of quietness and stillness so their spiritual ears are prepared to hear again?

Chapter Four

MISCONCEPTIONS ABOUT FULFILLMENT

The moment a poison is termed as food, you will feel comfortable taking it. This is what the devil seeks to achieve by redefining what fulfillment really means. " - Rev. Dr. Nadine Nkulu

The most dangerous trick of the devil is not always to push people into apparent disobedience. Sometimes, he shifts the definitions. He changes the meaning of things that matter. He makes sin look normal. He makes righteousness look strange. He wraps rebellion in the cloth of freedom. And he gives a new label to what should be avoided. When this shift happens, people no longer run from danger. They now run into it with boldness, thinking they are still walking in truth. That is how he defeats many believers.

In the beginning, the serpent did not force Eve to eat the fruit. He simply gave her a new understanding. He said, "God doth know that in the day ye eat thereof, then your eyes shall be opened, and ye shall be as gods, knowing good and evil." That was a redefinition.

He took something God called death and called it enlightenment. Once Eve accepted the new meaning, the next step was easy. She ate it. That is how spiritual deception works. It begins with a shift in definition. Once the heart believes a lie, the body will follow.

One of the key areas where this shift occurs is in the concept of fulfillment. The devil has worked hard to redefine what it means to be fulfilled. He has painted a picture that looks good, feels right, and sounds attractive. But it is not the picture God painted. It is a distortion. A twisted mirror. It reflects something, but not the truth.

In today's world, fulfillment has become closely tied to material success. When people say someone is fulfilled, they are often referring to aspects such as money, fame, status, marriage, children, or achievements. The measure is physical. The proof is visible. If you have more, then you must be fulfilled. If you have less, then something must be missing. This kind of thinking has crept into the hearts of many believers. Without realizing it, they now define fulfillment by worldly standards.

In Luke 12, Jesus tells a parable of a rich man whose land brought forth a plentiful harvest. The man said within himself,

"I will pull down my barns, and build greater; and there will I bestow all my fruits and my goods. And I will say to my soul, Soul, thou hast much goods laid up for many years; take thine ease, eat, drink, and be merry."

This man believed he was fulfilled. He had reached a point where he could rest and enjoy. But the voice of God came that same night, saying,

"Thou fool, this night thy soul shall be required of thee: then whose shall those things be, which thou hast provided?"

The issue here was not his wealth. It was his definition. He tied his soul to his possession. He thought rest and fulfillment came from barns, not from God. That night, he realized how wrong he was. But it was too late.

There was another man in Mark 10. He was rich and young. He came running to Jesus and asked what he must do to inherit eternal life. Jesus told him to keep the commandments, and he said he had done that from his youth. Then Jesus looked at him and loved him, and said, "One thing thou lackest: go thy way, sell whatsoever thou hast, and give to the poor, and thou shalt have treasure in heaven: and come, take up the cross, and follow me."

The man went away grieved, for he had great possessions. He was good in his own eyes. He had wealth and morality. But Jesus pointed at something more profound. His sense of fulfillment was rooted in his riches. When Jesus touched it, he chose the gold over the cross.

So many people are still living in that place today. They come to church, they read the Bible, but their hearts are tied to the world's mirror of fulfillment. They feel better when their bank account is full. They feel worse when it is not. They feel secure when life is working out. They feel abandoned when it is not. What the devil does is to press on this desire. He whispers, "You will be fulfilled when you get that job." "When you get married." "When you buy that house." "When people respect you." "When you reach your goals." And people chase these things with all their strength, only to find out that it does not satisfy the soul.

In Ecclesiastes 2, Solomon gave a full report of his pursuit. He said he made great works. He built houses. He planted vineyards. He gathered silver and gold. He got servants and singers and every delight of men. And then he said,

"Then I looked on all the works that my hands had wrought, and on the labour that I had laboured to do: and, behold, all was vanity and vexation of spirit, and there was no profit under the sun."

That is not a confession from a poor man. It is the voice of someone who had everything but still felt empty. Because true fulfillment does not come from what a man has, it comes from who he belongs to.

The devil undermines intimacy with God by replacing it with a focus on achievement. He tells people that they need to do more, get more, rise higher. And the more they pursue this, the further they drift from the place of intimacy. It is not always that they fall into sin. Sometimes, they fall into success. However, success can be a trap if it replaces surrender. That is why the misconception about fulfillment is dangerous. It shifts attention. It replaces presence with performance. It makes people forget the voice of the Shepherd because they are chasing the echo of applause.

When people accept this false definition, their relationship with God becomes performance-based. They pray to get things, not to grow. They study to preach, not to understand. They serve to be seen, not to be shaped. And slowly, their intimacy dies. They still have the language of faith, but they have lost the hunger. That is how people get lost in the shadows. They are still in the house, but the fire is gone.

In Matthew 6, Jesus gave a very different picture of fulfillment. He said, "Lay not up for yourselves treasures upon earth, where moth and rust doth corrupt, and where thieves break through and steal: But lay up for yourselves treasures in heaven."

He warned that where a man's treasure is, there will his heart be also. Fulfillment is not about storage. It is about location. If a man's heart is in heaven, then his fulfillment is safe. But if it is tied to earthly things, then it is vulnerable.

Paul gave another deep insight in Philippians 4. He said, "I have learned, in whatsoever state I am, therewith to be content." He had been abased and abounded. He had been full and hungry. But none of these states defined him. His fulfillment was not in his status. It was in Christ. That is why he could say in verse 13,

"I can do all things through Christ, which strengtheneth me."

That strength came from intimacy. Not position. The enemy wants to disconnect people from this truth. He wants them to measure life by what they have, what they feel, or how people see them. That way, they become restless. Always chasing and never arriving. Always hungry. Never satisfied. But when fulfillment is redefined as knowing God and walking with Him, peace follows. Even in hard times. Even in the wilderness.

There was a man called Asaph. In Psalm 73, he confessed that he was envious of the wicked. He saw their prosperity. He saw how they seemed free from trouble. And he began to wonder if serving God was in vain. But then he said,

"Until I went into the sanctuary of God; then understood I their end."

He realized that what appeared to be fulfillment was actually emptiness. Then he said something powerful in verse 25,

"Whom have I in heaven but thee? and there is none upon earth that I desire beside thee."

That is true fulfillment when God becomes the desire. Not things. Not status. Not comfort. Just Him.

True fulfillment can never be built on things that fade. The moment your sense of value is tied to the visible, you become unstable. That is why many people today live in silent frustration. They are tired, but they cannot explain why. Blessings surround them, but they still feel something is missing. It is because their soul is still hungry. And only God can satisfy it. The devil's trick is to keep them distracted long enough until their hunger becomes confusion.

Some people feel fulfilled when they are applauded. They live off compliments. Their energy comes from attention. But that kind of fulfillment is dangerous. Because when the crowd stops clapping, they collapse. Jesus never trusted the crowd. He did not commit Himself unto them because He knew what was in man. That shows something important. Not every hand clap is a confirmation. And not every silence means absence. If you know who you are in God, you will not need constant praise to stay encouraged.

CHASING FEELINGS, NOT THE FATHER

"If someone builds his relationship with God based on emotions, he will find himself sinking when the winds of life blow."- Rev Dr. Nadine Nkulu

Many people today believe they are fulfilled because their emotions lead them to think so. They confuse emotional highs with spiritual depth. This is not new. Even in the days of the prophets, Israel often rejoiced in the wrong things. In Amos chapter 5:21-23, the Lord said,

"I hate, I despise your feast days, and I will not smell in your solemn assemblies. Though ye offer me burnt offerings and your meat offerings, I will not accept them."

They were celebrating. They felt good. However, God was not a part of their celebration. Their emotions were high, but their spirits were low. They chased feelings, not the Father.

The world today teaches that fulfillment is found in being happy. It says one should do what feels right. However, the Bible never instructs anyone to follow their heart. Instead, it says in Proverbs 28:26,

"He that trusteth in his own heart is a fool: but whoso walketh wisely, he shall be delivered."

God knows that the heart can deceive. He knows that feelings can lie. That is why He called men to follow Him, not follow what feels good. Jesus never said, "Come and feel better." He said, "Follow Me." The call was never to chase happiness. It was to chase holiness.

There is a concept that many do not realize they have accepted. It is the idea of chasing the wrong signal. A signal in itself is not the destination. It only points to something. A red traffic light signals to stop. However, if a driver obeys the light without knowing their destination, they may keep stopping and moving without ever arriving. Some people have turned goosebumps during worship into their destination. Others treat answered prayer as the final sign that they are right with God. But even the devil can mimic results. What he cannot mimic is true intimacy with the Father. Feelings may come and go. What remains is a consistent walk with the Spirit.

Why does the devil target emotions so strongly? Because he knows they are powerful. He knows that what a person feels can guide what he does. If he can hijack a person's emotions, he can hijack his journey. He does not need to tempt someone with sin directly. He only needs to twist the person's definition of fulfillment. He may convince someone that serving in church means God is pleased, even if the person's heart is far from God. That person will then chase performance instead of presence. He will seek crowds instead of Christ. This is why Paul warned Timothy in 2 Timothy 4:3 that the time would come when people would not endure sound doctrine but would, after their own lusts, heap to themselves teachers, having itching ears. That itching is a feeling. And that feeling pushes them away from truth. The devil loves to make people feel good about what is not godly. He wraps danger in delight. He puts poison in pretty packages.

There is also a very subtle exchange that happens in the heart. A person may begin by genuinely seeking God. But over time, he begins to measure his growth by how he feels. He thinks he has grown spiritually because he cries during worship. He assumes he is closer to God because he got a promotion at work. These are wrong indicators. They are signals that do not always lead to the right place. And when someone follows the wrong signal long enough, he ends up in a dry place, wondering how he got there.

Many times, people replace God's commendation with man's applause. They want to be seen. They want to be celebrated. And in doing so, they slowly shift from pleasing God to impressing men. That shift is dangerous. Jesus said in John chapter 5 verse 44,

"How can ye believe, which receive honour one of another, and seek not the honour that cometh from God only?"

If someone is chasing compliments from men, he is no longer chasing the heart of the Father. That pursuit will lead him far from true fulfillment.

The problem is that feelings can be spiritual but not divine. A person may feel a spiritual pull and assume it is from God, but not all spirits are holy. That is why John said in 1 John chapter 4 verse 1,

"Beloved, believe not every spirit, but try the spirits whether they are of God."

If someone does not test the origin of what they feel, they may end up embracing what destroys them. Many have walked into emotional traps because they failed to check the source of their excitement.

When a believer begins to think that fulfillment is found in how well things are going, or how excited they feel during service, or how emotional they get during prayer, they are setting themselves up for disappointment. That person will struggle in dry seasons. He will feel empty when life gets hard because his joy was never rooted in the Father. It was rooted in feelings. David understood this well. That is why he said in Psalm 63:1,

"O God, thou art my God; early will I seek thee: my soul thirsteth for thee."

He did not thirst for what God could give. He thirsted for God

Himself.

The danger of this emotion-driven faith is that it does not last. It is like the seed in the parable of the sower that fell on stony ground. It sprang up quickly with joy, but when trouble came, it withered. Because it had no depth. That is what chasing feelings produces—shallow roots. No strength. No endurance. And no intimacy. God is not a feeling. He is a person—a real being. And a real relationship with Him will not always feel exciting. Sometimes it feels like silence. Sometimes it feels like pain. But it is still real. And it is still fulfilling.

If someone builds their life on what they feel, they are building on sand. The storm will come. And when it does, only the house built on the rock will stand. Jesus is the rock. Not emotion. Not experience. Not even results. Just Him. Chasing Him is the only way to remain stable. Feelings will fade. But the Father remains the same.

The devil uses feelings because they are easier to manipulate. He knows people trust what they feel more than what they believe. So, he feeds their feelings until they can no longer hear the voice of truth. He keeps them busy chasing moments instead of building communion. He keeps them addicted to spiritual highs so they never develop proper discipline. He knows that emotional faith does not endure trials. That kind of faith dies when God seems silent.

There are moments when intimacy with God feels dry. There are seasons when a believer does not feel goosebumps during prayer. That does not mean God has gone. It means the relationship is going deeper. It is moving beyond emotion into covenant. But if someone has been trained to think that God is only present when he feels something, he will run away during those dry seasons. He will seek another feeling to replace what he has lost. And the devil will be ready with a distraction.

It is essential to understand that God is not opposed to feelings. He created them. But they were never meant to lead. They were meant to follow. The spirit should lead. The soul should obey. And the body should submit. When someone allows his feelings to lead, he turns that order upside down. That is rebellion, even if it looks spiritual. True fulfillment is found when the spirit leads, guided by the word of God.

There is a better way. It is the way of quiet consistency. Of steady communion. Of trusting God even when the heart is confused. Of walking by faith, not by sight. Of loving God, not because it feels good, but because He is worthy. That kind of life is not loud. It is not always exciting. But it lasts.

MISTAKING PERFORMANCE FOR PRESENCE

"One of the ways the enemy leads people away from God is by separating them from presence while leaving the structure of performance untouched." - Rev Dr. Nadine Nkulu

The enemy does not mind when people keep doing church so long as they stop being the church. He does not oppose the performance so long as presence has departed. And the most dangerous part is that sometimes presence can depart, and performance can continue without interruption. The crowd claps. The voice still sounds good. The stage still looks full. But heaven has left the building.

Cain was a man who brought an offering to God. From the outside, it appeared to be good. He gave something. He sacrificed. He showed up with an act of devotion. "But God had no respect unto Cain and to his offering." There was performance but no approval. Presence did not descend. And when his act was not accepted, instead of adjusting himself, Cain got angry. Genesis chapter four reveals a man more committed to the act than the heart behind the act. He was not sensitive to presence. He cared more for the acceptance of his activity than for alignment with God's instruction.

The flesh likes routine. It prefers to do something that appears religious because that feels measurable. It is easier to keep count of prayers than to discern brokenness. It is easier to look for goosebumps than to genuinely seek God's voice. It is easier to shout in worship than to surrender in silence. And this is why many keep the motions going, but the spirit is no longer engaged. A person can sing about surrender and never surrender. They can preach about obedience and still live in rebellion because performance can continue when presence is absent.

The tabernacle of Moses had many items and a detailed order. There was the outer court, the inner court, and the most holy place. Only one carried the presence. The others were important, but the place where God met with man was the most sacred. Yet when the people rebelled and went their own way, the glory departed. Ichabod was declared. The glory was gone, but the tent remained. The people still had the furniture, but not the fellowship. And that is how many live today. They have the form of godliness but deny the power. They keep the instruments of worship but lose the intimacy of worship.

In First Samuel chapter four, the children of Israel brought the ark of God into battle as though it were a magical object. They shouted. They were excited. They thought victory was guaranteed. But God did not go with them. Because the presence cannot be manipulated. And when God is not present, noise will not save. There was performance on the battlefield but no presence. They had assumed that carrying the ark automatically meant God would fight. But the relationship had been broken, and no amount of performance could replace presence.

Even in the New Testament, Jesus rebuked the Pharisees for this very thing. He said in Matthew chapter fifteen,

"These people draw nigh unto me with their mouth and honour me with their lips, but their heart is far from me. But in vain they do worship me, teaching for doctrines the commandments of men."

It means people can be involved in worship and still be far. They can recite the words and still miss the heart. They can shout Jesus and still not know Him. That is what performance without presence produces.

People are taught to value what can be measured. That is why a person may feel more spiritual when they cry, fall, or experience some warmth during worship. But scripture never said feelings are the proof of presence. It said in John chapter one, "In the beginning was the Word." It never said, "In the beginning was the feeling." It means a person may feel nothing and still be in deep fellowship. And they may feel everything and still be lost in deception. Feelings are not the standard. The Word is.

Sometimes, presence will lead you away from the crowd. It will take you to a private place. When Moses met God at the burning bush, it was not in a temple. It was in the wilderness. When Jacob wrestled with God, it was at night and alone. When Paul encountered Jesus, it was on a lonely road. Presence is personal before it is public. It touches the inside before it flows outside. It deals with the heart before it anoints the hand. And that is why a person can lay hands on the sick and see healing and still be far from God. Because gifts are not proof of closeness. The Corinthian church had all the gifts, yet Paul said they were carnal.

The devil does not mind if a person speaks in tongues so long as their heart is proud. He does not fear the raising of hands if the life is full of sin. He does not tremble at the sound of worship songs if there is no obedience behind it. What makes hell nervous is not activity. It is authenticity. It is not loudness. It is alignment.

The modern church must return to this truth. There must be a hunger for what is real. There must be a hunger for the Word, not just a manifestation. There must be a desire for obedience, not just excitement, because presence is holy. It does not dwell where compromise is celebrated. It does not remain where pride is tolerated. It does not rest where performance has taken the throne. If a person wants presence, they must invite truth. And the truth is not always convenient. It will confront. It will correct. It will cleanse. But in that cleansing is the invitation to deeper intimacy.

Presence is not an accident. It is the reward of pursuit. It is not about getting a feeling. It is about surrendering fully. That is why the early church in Acts chapter two did not just gather for show. They continued steadfastly in the apostle's doctrine and fellowship and in breaking of bread and in prayers. It was a devotion that birthed manifestation. It was a unity that invited presence. And because the foundation was right, the fire could fall. If people want true revival, they must desire the God of revival more than the sound of it. They must seek His Word more than the wonders.

Even when David danced before the Lord with all his might, it was not for the people. It was for the Lord. He was king, but he humbled himself. And when his wife mocked him, he said in Second Samuel chapter six, It was before the Lord. His worship was not a performance. It was intimacy. It was affection expressed in humility. And because it was genuine, it drew presence.

In this generation, there must be a return to the place of presence. Men must learn to discern when God is truly present and when it is just the noise of performance. And that discernment comes from knowing the Word. Hebrews 4 says,

"The Word of God is quick and powerful and sharper than any two-edged sword piercing even to the dividing asunder of soul and spirit."

It means the Word can separate emotion from truth. It can reveal whether a person is in the presence or just lost in performance.

There is no substitute for presence. No amount of lights, sounds, or structure can replace it. When God is present, lives are transformed. Hearts are healed. Chains are broken. But when performance is all that remains, people will clap and go home empty. They will dance and still remain in bondage. They will shout "Amen!" and still be dead on the inside because only presence brings life. And that life comes when the heart is open, and the Word is honored.

DISCUSSION QUESTIONS

1. Where do you personally feel the most "noise" in life right now?

2. What's one thing that tends to distract you from hearing God clearly?

3. How do you usually know when your heart is getting cluttered or overwhelmed?

4. Have you ever mistaken busyness for spiritual health? What did that look like?

5. What helps you slow down enough to reconnect with God when life feels chaotic?

6. Can you think of a time when God was speaking, but life's noise made it hard to notice?

7. What is one simple change you could make this week to create more quiet space for God?

Chapter Five

THE WOUNDED HEART
AND THE SILENT GAP

*T*he heart becomes wounded when it strives to get by man's effort, what only grace can give." - Rev. Dr. Nadine Nkulu

From the beginning, man has always struggled to relate to God from a place of performance. Even in the wilderness, the children of Israel could not understand a relationship based on trust. In Exodus 19:8, when Moses brought the word of the Lord to the people, they answered,

"All that the Lord hath spoken we will do."

Their hearts were quick to commit to doing, not because they understood what God wanted, but because they assumed that doing was the pathway to receiving. God had just delivered them from bondage by grace, without any merit from them. Yet, they immediately shifted into a transactional mindset. This is the beginning of the wounded heart.

When people enter a relationship with God, thinking that it is their effort that keeps them close, they are setting themselves up for disappointment. This was the root of the law. The people wanted rules they could follow to keep God happy. They wanted measurable works. So, God gave them the Law through Moses. But the Law was never the true solution. Romans 3:20 says,

"Therefore by the deeds of the law there shall no flesh be justified in his sight: for by the law is the knowledge of sin."

The Law made men aware of their inability to meet God's standard. It exposed their weakness. But instead of freeing them, it created a gap. It made them more conscious of their efforts than God's grace. Over time, this led to wounded hearts.

The heart becomes wounded when it strives for what only grace can give. This is the silent pain that many believers endure. They pray, fast, give, and serve, but they still feel far from God. They compare their service to their results and wonder why things are not aligning. They get offended, not outwardly, but internally. Something in them says, "I have done all I can, yet God is silent." That silence becomes a gap. They begin to question the love of God. The enemy takes advantage of this silence. He whispers, "You are not good enough. If you prayed more, you would be heard. If you gave more, you would be blessed." Without realizing it, the person shifts even deeper into performance, even deeper into striving. And the heart, quietly, bleeds.

God never designed relationship with Him to be based on works. From the Garden of Eden, it was always about presence and communion. When Adam sinned, it was not his nakedness that made God distance Himself. In fact, God came looking for him, saying,

"Adam, where art thou?" (Genesis 3:9).

That question was not about location; it was about intimacy. God was asking, "Where is our fellowship? Where is the place where we used to meet?" Sin had broken it, not works. And ever since then, man has sought to earn God's presence through effort.

The Old Testament repeatedly illustrates this pattern. Men trying to win God's favor by sacrifice, by obedience to laws, by acts of service. Yet, in Hosea 6:6, God said,

"For I desired mercy, and not sacrifice; and the knowledge of

God more than burnt offerings."

God was never primarily looking for what man could do. He was looking for a heart that knew Him. The knowledge of God, not through feeling, but through His word. This is where intimacy is found.

To measure intimacy with God, one must examine one's relationship with the word. Is the word of God alive in his heart? Does he hunger for it like daily bread? Psalm 119:105 says,

"Thy word is a lamp unto my feet, and a light unto my path."

Without the word, a person walks in darkness, regardless of how active they are in the church. The word reveals God's mind. It is not an emotional tool; it is the compass of relationship.

Paul understood this. In Philippians 3, he listed all his achievements under the law. He was a Hebrew of Hebrews, a Pharisee, blameless in the law. Yet in verse 7, he said,

"But what things were gain to me, those I counted loss for Christ."

He realized that all his performance could not earn him intimacy. In verse 10, he declared his heart's cry,

"That I may know him."

Not that I may work for Him, but that I may know Him. This is the shift God calls every believer to make, from doing to knowing.

A person must be willing to stop proving their love to God by acts, and instead, embrace the love God has already given. Romans 5:8 says,

"But God commendeth his love toward us, in that, while we were yet sinners, Christ died for us."

This love was not based on merit. It was given when man had nothing to offer. That is the foundation of true fulfillment.

When the heart is always in performance mode, it becomes exhausted. The person begins to experience spiritual fatigue. They still show up, but they are no longer present. They serve, but they feel empty. They give but feel used. Eventually, they grow bitter. They see others who do less seemingly receive more, and they wonder why God is unfair. But the problem is not God's fairness. The problem is that they built their relationship with God on works rather than grace.

Every believer must ask themselves, 'Why am I doing what I am doing?' Is it to gain God's approval, or because I already have it? Intimacy is not about doing more; it is about drawing near. James 4:8 says, "Draw nigh to God, and he will draw nigh to you." It is a posture of the heart. A broken heart does not need more activity; it needs truth. And the truth is that God never asked for performance. He asked for presence.

God did not make us workers first. He made us sons. Romans 8:15 says,

"For ye have not received the spirit of bondage again to fear; but ye have received the Spirit of adoption, whereby we cry, Abba, Father."

This is not the language of servants. It is the cry of sons. Sons do not earn an inheritance. They receive it by birth. God is not looking for laborers without relationship. He is seeking intimacy that produces fruitful service, not the other way around.

In churches, people are applauded for their service. But heaven does not count hours served. Heaven looks at the heart behind the service. In Matthew 7:22-23, Jesus said,

"Many will say to me in that day, Lord, Lord, have we not prophesied in thy name? and in thy name have cast out devils? And in thy name done many wonderful works?"

These people were engaged in works. But Jesus responded,

"I never knew you: depart from me, ye that work iniquity."

That word "knew" means intimate relationship. They did things in His name, but never knew Him. This is the ultimate silent gap.

PAIN, DISAPPOINTMENT, AND WITHDRAWING FROM GOD

"God did not call man to impress Him. He called man to walk with Him. There is a difference between impressing and walking." - Rev Dr. Nadine Nkulu

A man who approaches God from the mindset of works will always end up in pain. He may not see it immediately. In fact, it may take years of faithful service, long hours of prayer, and consistent giving before the cracks begin to show. But the pain comes. It always does. That is because the foundation is faulty. When a man builds his relationship with God on what he does for God rather than on who God is and what God has already done in Christ, he sets himself up for heartbreak.

God did not call man to impress Him. He called man to walk with Him. There is a difference between performance and fellowship. There is a difference between impressing and walking. God is not asking for display; He is seeking worship in spirit and in truth. Jesus said in John 4:23,

"But the hour cometh, and now is, when the true worshippers shall worship the Father in spirit and in truth: for the Father seeketh such to worship him."

This means God already has a pattern, a way He wants to be approached. And it is not through works of the law.

The painful reality is that many people do not realize they have substituted worship with labor. They think God is asking them to keep doing things to prove their faith. So, they pile up religious activities and call it devotion. They believe their prayers keep them saved. They believe their long fasts make them more righteous. But slowly, disappointment starts to build because their expectations are not met. They expect results from God that He never promised. When those expectations are not met, pain follows.

Take, for example, a man who believes that his personal discipline, including waking up every night at 12 to pray, fasting twice a week, and giving to every cause, is what keeps him right with God. At first, he feels confident. He is doing something. He is staying on fire. But then he sees someone else who does not do any of those things, yet that person receives favor, walks in peace, and lives with joy. Suddenly, confusion sets in. Instead of joy, envy begins to grow. Instead of peace, resentment forms. That man begins to feel ignored, overlooked, and abandoned by God. Not because God failed, but because the man's foundation was not grace. It was works.

Pain enters when expectations are built on human performance. Proverbs 13:12 says,

"Hope deferred maketh the heart sick: but when the desire cometh, it is a tree of life."

When someone builds hope around something God never

promised, the delay or failure of that thing produces pain. Not just emotional pain, but spiritual discouragement as well. The person begins to question the goodness of God. He feels let down by the very One he served. And then comes the most dangerous step, which is withdrawal.

Withdrawal from God is often quiet. It typically does not begin with a loud announcement. The person does not wake up one day and say he is done with God. It is more subtle. He stops praying with joy. His Bible reading becomes mechanical. He no longer expects answers from God. He still goes to church, still lifts his hands in worship, but his heart is distant. He is there, but not really present. He is speaking the words, but the faith is gone. This is how many believers lose their walk with God without ever realizing it. They are still busy, still around, but their spirit has drifted.

In the book of Luke, the elder brother in the parable of the prodigal son is a good example. He never left the house. He never squandered his inheritance. But when his brother returned, and the father threw a celebration, his heart was exposed. He said in Luke 15:29,

"Lo, these many years do I serve thee, neither transgressed I at any time thy commandment: and yet thou never gavest me a kid, that I might make merry with my friends."

That was the language of pain. That was the voice of disappointment. He had served, obeyed, done all the right things, yet he felt unrewarded. The bitterness had been building, silently, until it erupted. His issue was not his brother's return. His issue was with the father. He could not understand how grace could be given so freely when he had worked so hard.

This is where many believers find themselves. They served with sincerity. They gave with sacrifice. They fasted with tears. But when their reward did not come as they expected, or when someone else received it sooner, they withdrew in their hearts. And slowly, they shifted from worship to entitlement. They began to serve God for what they could get, not because of who He is. And when the getting stopped, the serving lost its meaning.

God has never been moved by works. Even under the old

covenant, He made it clear that He valued obedience from the heart more than rituals. In 1 Samuel 15:22, Samuel told Saul,

"Hath the Lord as great delight in burnt offerings and sacrifices, as in obeying the voice of the Lord? Behold, to obey is better than sacrifice."

God wanted relationship. He wanted trust. But man kept defaulting to performance. It felt safer. It felt measurable. But it never produced intimacy.

Disappointment becomes even more painful when the believer begins to compare his life with others. Comparison adds fuel to the fire. The person starts to say things like, "I have been in church longer than him," or "I have prayed more than her," or "Why does she get that breakthrough while I am still struggling?" These thoughts breed offense. Not just against people, but against God. A quiet accusation forms in the heart: "God is not fair." That accusation, if unchecked, can lead to bitterness.

Bitterness is the seed of rebellion. A person who was once humble and teachable now becomes cold and sarcastic. He may still speak Christian language, but the warmth is gone. He might say "Glory to God" with his lips, but his heart is not in it. He has withdrawn. He is present, but not connected.

The worst part of this withdrawal is that it often leads people to chase shadows. If they do not leave God entirely, they begin to pursue things God never gave. They start chasing a version of success that is built on assumptions. They chase a promise God never spoke. And because they believe it was God who promised it, they wait endlessly, hoping it will come to pass. And when it does not come, they sink deeper into disappointment. They are no longer worshiping God; they are worshiping an outcome.

When expectations are built on assumptions instead of the written word, it opens the door to deception. The serpent in the garden never told Eve to abandon God. He only twisted the meaning of what God said. That is how disappointment begins—a twisted version of God's promise. A person starts to assume that because they serve faithfully, God is obligated to do what they imagine. They do not realize that service to God is never a contract. It is a relationship of trust. When service becomes a transaction, God is no longer worshiped; He is negotiated with.

This is why many believers silently stop trusting God, even though they still use His name. They sing about faith but no longer believe. They talk about peace but carry silent anger. Their service continues, but the connection is broken. At the root of that disconnection is a wound. Pain unchecked becomes a wound, and that wound becomes a silent reason for spiritual withdrawal.

Withdrawal is not always immediately visible. It may look like reduced joy. It may sound like shorter prayers. It may manifest as a lack of excitement about things of God. But beneath all that is a deep pain, a hurt that says, "God did not do what I expected." When that pain is not healed, it becomes disappointment. And when disappointment lingers, it affects how that person sees God.

Scripture never promised a pain-free life. In fact, Jesus said in John 16:33,

"In the world ye shall have tribulation: but be of good cheer; I have overcome the world."

God never promised a smooth road. He promised His presence. That is the promise; Himself. When people expect what He never promised, they prepare their hearts for heartbreak.

WHEN GOD FEELS SILENT

"The greatest test of man's loyalty is what he does when God is silent." - Rev Dr. Nadine Nkulu

The seasons where God feels silent are the most sensitive parts of any walk with Him. Nothing confuses a sincere heart more than silence after obedience. The soul expects an answer, a sign, a voice, or some confirmation, but instead it hears nothing. And when this silence continues, it becomes a heavy burden. Yet, even in silence, God has not left. Silence is not absence. It never was.

Scripture reveals many instances where God remained silent, not because He turned away, but because He was engaged in something more profound. One of the most striking examples is found in the story of Job. Job lost almost everything: his children, his possessions, and his health. His friends came and spoke many words, and Job himself cried out in anguish. But God remained silent for most of the book. He only responded towards the end, after Job had poured out all his confusion and pain. This tells us something important. The silence of God is not always about what we did wrong. Sometimes it is about what He is building in us.

The most significant test of man's loyalty is what he does when God is silent. When the voice of heaven seems to stop speaking, many people turn to the voice of man or the voice of emotions. They fill the silence with activity, advice, and assumptions. But silence should lead to stillness, not noise. Psalm 46:10 says,

"Be still, and know that I am God."

Stillness is not laziness. It is a posture of trust. It is a refusal to replace God's voice with alternatives.

When man leans too heavily on his own works, it becomes harder to hear God. Israel in the Old Testament was deeply committed to rituals. They offered sacrifices, observed feasts, and adhered to traditions. But in Isaiah chapter 1, God said, "Bring no more vain oblations; incense is an abomination unto me."

He was not rejecting worship. He was rejecting performance without relationship. They were so committed to doing things for God that they forgot to walk with God. And in that busyness, they could no longer hear Him. This same pattern is still evident today.

When desires become the loudest voice, the voice of God becomes secondary. It is not that God stops speaking. It is that man stops listening. He filters everything through what he wants to hear. He prays with a list, not a heart. He worships with an agenda, not adoration. And slowly, he begins to feel abandoned. But God never left. The issue is the heart.

In the wilderness, Israel heard the voice of God through Moses. But they did not want to hear God for themselves. In Exodus 20:19, they said,

"Speak thou with us, and we will hear: but let not God speak with us, lest we die."

They feared intimacy. They preferred distance. They wanted instructions, not relationship. This pattern followed them for generations. And as they moved further into works and rituals, they grew deaf to grace.

Grace speaks a different language. It does not shout. It does not rush. It invites. But if the heart is already full, there is no room for invitation. When a person is full of ambition, even good things can become distractions. The voice of grace becomes strange to a heart that is used to earning. And so, when God offers rest, they reject it. Not because they hate God, but because they do not know how to relate to a God who gives freely.

The New Testament brought a new language. God sent His Son, not a list. He gave a person, not a program. But many still preferred the old system. Even after Jesus came, some still wanted to mix grace with law. Paul wrote strongly about this. In Galatians 5:4, he said,

"Christ is become of no effect unto you, whosoever of you are justified by the law; ye are fallen from grace."

The moment a person depends on works, the effect of Christ is lost in their life.

This is not just about doctrine. It affects how people hear God. A person who depends on performance will only expect God to speak when they have done something right. And when they feel unworthy, they expect silence. But God's silence is not always linked to sin. Sometimes it is related to maturity. He wants us to trust Him even when we do not hear Him.

David had moments when God seemed far away. In Psalm 13:1, he cried,

"How long wilt thou forget me, O Lord? Forever? How long wilt thou hide thy face from me?"

This was the man after God's heart. He was not a stranger to God's presence. But even he experienced silence. That silence did not mean rejection. It was a space where his trust was put to the test.

Silence often feels like emptiness, but it is actually space. Space for reflection. Space for purification. Space for realignment. When everything is loud, it is hard to see clearly. But in silence, hidden motives come to the surface. The heart is exposed. The questions become sharper. The need for control is confronted. And slowly, the soul learns to rest.

God's silence trains the ear. It makes the heart sensitive. When the loud voices stop, the soul starts to notice whispers again. That is how relationship grows. Not just by constant talking, but by shared presence. Two truly close people can sit in silence without discomfort. That is the goal of intimacy: to be so rooted in trust that silence does not feel like abandonment.

Jesus Himself experienced silence. In the garden of Gethsemane, He prayed three times, asking the Father to take away the cup. But there was no voice from heaven. No angel appeared with a message. He received strength, but not an answer. And still, He said, Thy will be done. That silence was not rejection. It was trust.

Many believers have not been taught how to trust God in silence. They think God only speaks when things are good. But genuine faith is built when things are quiet. When there is no voice, no sign, and no feeling, but the heart still says, I believe. That is worship. That is surrender.

Silence can also expose idolatry. When God does not speak, some people quickly turn to other sources of guidance. They run to prophets, to dreams, to strange voices. Not because they are hungry, but because they are impatient. They want answers more than presence. And in that rush, they open the door to deception.

The story of King Saul shows this clearly. In 1 Samuel 28, Saul sought God, but God did not answer him. Instead of waiting or repenting, he went to a witch. He wanted results, not relationship. And that decision sealed his downfall. Silence revealed his heart. It showed that he valued answers more than obedience.

The voice of God is not always a sound. Sometimes it is a sense. Sometimes it is a stillness. Sometimes it is a scripture that comes alive. But if the heart is restless, even the most unmistakable voice will sound like silence. God is not always loud. He often waits until the noise inside us fades.

There is a beauty in silence. It creates space for God to move in ways we did not expect. It removes distractions. It breaks dependence on feelings. And it teaches the heart to rest, not just to react. But only those who stay long enough in silence will see its treasure.

DISCUSSION QUESTIONS

1. Where do you see yourself slipping into "performance mode" with God without realizing it?

2. Why do you think so many believers today feel pressure to earn God's approval?

3. Have you ever felt disappointed with God because your effort didn't match your results? What did that feel like?

4. How can we tell when we're doing things for God instead of walking with God?

5. Where have you personally felt the quiet pain of striving instead of resting in grace?

6. What helps you shift from "trying harder" to actually trusting God?

7. How can we support each other in our small group to move from performance to intimacy with God?

Chapter Six

FACING THE INNER IDOL

*I*dolatry today is more about what sits on the throne of a person's heart than what sits on a shelf." - Rev. Dr. Nadine Nkulu

The greatest idol is not what is placed in a corner but what is placed at the center of a person's desire. And the most deceptive part of it is that most people are unaware that they are worshiping an idol. They do not recognize that what they are passionately pursuing is something they have placed above God. The Bible clearly shows that God not only wants to be worshiped outwardly, but that He demands full ownership of the heart. He told His people,

"Thou shalt have no other gods before me" (Exodus 20:3).

This command was not limited to physical gods. It included anything or anyone that would compete with God for attention, devotion, and love.

In today's world, the idol is often internal. It is not a statue but a strong desire. It is not a symbol but a silent voice within. It may take the shape of ambition, dreams, personal success, self-image, or even spiritual achievement. These things are not sinful in themselves. But they become idols when they become the reason for living, the thing one cannot give up, the desire that drives one more than a desire for God. Many Christians unknowingly have made their dreams more important than their intimacy with God. They wake up each day with their goals in mind, but leave their Bibles unopened. They attend meetings and pursue projects, but neglect the secret place. Their entire spiritual discipline becomes a means to fuel their own ambition.

The inner idol hides behind good things. It never presents itself as evil. It takes advantage of what is acceptable. It uses the mask of success, progress, or even ministry. A person can chase after ministry and call it purpose, while God is being slowly replaced by the very work that is meant to serve Him. This is what happened to Saul. God chose him to be king, but along the way, he began to desire the praise of men more than the approval of God. In 1 Samuel 15:24, Saul confessed to Samuel, saying,

"I have sinned: for I have transgressed the commandment of the Lord, and thy words: because I feared the people, and obeyed their voice."

That was a clear exposure of the inner idol. Saul was led by the fear of man, not by the fear of God.

The inner idol does not show itself quickly. It is silent, but it demands worship. It tells people they must be something, they must reach somewhere, they must accomplish more. And the moment one begins to feel like their worth is found in their achievements, they have entered into idolatry. They are no longer serving God but serving the shadow of what they think they must become. It is dangerous because it looks harmless. It keeps a person busy but spiritually dry. It keeps a person moving but disconnected from God. It makes a person perform without presence.

Jesus warned about this kind of heart when He said,

"For where your treasure is, there will your heart be also" (Matthew 6:21).

He was pointing out that what one values most is what occupies the heart. And whatever occupies the heart above God is an idol.

Many have unknowingly allowed their expectations to take the place of God. They have prayed not to know God but to use Him to achieve their goals. God becomes a means, not the end. That shift is where intimacy is lost.

An inner idol is difficult to confront because it feels right. It feels like one is on the right path. After all, they are pursuing good things. But the test is this: If God asks to take it away, can you still remain content? Abraham faced this test with Isaac. Isaac was not a graven image; he was a gift from God. Yet God asked Abraham to sacrifice him. Genesis 22 shows the painful obedience of a man who would not allow even the promise of God to become more important than God Himself. Abraham passed the test. He proved that even the best gift must not take the place of the Giver.

Today, people create their own Isaacs. They build dreams and attach God to them. But they cannot let it go if God says so. That is idolatry. The inner idol makes a person feel spiritual while they are still driven by themselves. They pray, they fast, but it is not for the pleasure of God. It is to push their vision. They do not want to wait for God's timing. They want results now. And so, they create a shadow. They chase the shadow of fulfillment. But no matter how fast they run, they find themselves exhausted, dissatisfied, and spiritually empty. The shadow can never satisfy.

In Ezekiel 14:3, the Lord said,

"Son of man, these men have set up their idols in their heart, and put the stumbling block of their iniquity before their face."

This verse reveals the truth that idols can be internal. These men were still in Israel. They were still part of the people of God. But they had erected idols in their hearts. These were not physical objects. They were inward loyalties. They were attachments, affections, and intentions that had replaced the desire for God.

Many people today are in the same situation. They attend church, they serve, they give, but their hearts are far from God. Their loyalty lies somewhere else. They claim to trust God, but they rely on their own strength. They speak of faith, but their decisions are driven by fear. They pray, but their prayer is more of manipulation than submission. All these are symptoms of inner idolatry. It is subtle, but it is dangerous.

Sometimes, this idolatry comes from unresolved identity issues. A person who never felt accepted now seeks validation through achievement. Another who was always overlooked now wants to prove a point. These wounds become the fuel behind the idol. They keep chasing success not because they love God, but because they want to silence the voice of insecurity. That pursuit becomes a form of worship. It replaces intimacy with performance. It replaces rest with restless ambition.

The danger of the inner idol is that it offers a false sense of fulfillment. It provides temporary satisfaction but ultimately leaves one feeling empty. One may feel happy after a promotion, but still feel dry inside. They may achieve a goal but still feel restless. That is because the soul was not designed to be satisfied by things. Only God satisfies the soul. The Psalmist said in Psalm 107:9,

"For he satisfieth the longing soul, and filleth the hungry soul with goodness."

People are often taught to dream big, pursue their desires, and never give up. However, they are rarely taught to surrender those dreams to God. The modern world celebrates the self-made person. It applauds independence. But the gospel calls for surrender. The gospel calls for a life that says,

"Not my will, but thine, be done" (Luke 22:42).

That kind of life is foreign to many believers today. They want God to support their plans, not interrupt them.

An example is a young man who pursued a career in music. He had talent, connections, and passion. He believed God gave him the gift. But over time, his gift became his god. He stopped praying unless it was for a breakthrough. He stopped reading the Word unless he was preparing a song. He stopped fellowshipping unless it was part of a concert. His life became centered around what he was becoming, not who he was with. God became distant. Yet he did not notice. He was still busy. He was still active. But he was lost in the shadow.

The shadow of the inner idol is exhausting. It keeps one working, but never allows one to rest. It keeps one doing, but never being.

It offers no peace. It only increases pressure. And the worst part is that it often hides behind spiritual language. One might say they are working for God when in fact they are working for their image. One might say they are pursuing purpose when in fact they are pursuing relevance. This is the silent trap.

The inner idol creates anxiety. It creates competition. It creates a false urgency. People start to compare their progress with that of others. They measure their value by the results they see. They feel left behind when others appear to be ahead. All these feelings come from worshiping the wrong thing. They no longer live to please God but to prove something. That shift is what kills intimacy.

The inner idol is a thief. It steals joy. It steals peace. It steals the voice of God. It replaces the still small voice with noise. It takes away the sweetness of fellowship and replaces it with deadlines. It replaces prayer with planning. It replaces listening with leading. It does not feel like rebellion, but it is. It does not feel like pride, but it is. It is a form of godliness without the power.

THE BATTLE OF SELF-RELIANCE

"Success is not always the signature of God. The real proof is dependence." - Rev Dr. Nadine Nkulu

Every adult must, at some point, learn to stand on their own feet, make wise decisions, and take responsibility for their actions. It is often praised as a sign of maturity, and rightly so. No one is expected to live a helpless life of dependency forever. From childhood, people are taught to clean up after themselves, to speak for themselves, and to navigate life. That is how society is built. There is value in learning how to solve problems, make plans, work hard, and create. Even Paul, the apostle, worked with his hands as a tentmaker and took pride in not being a burden to the churches. Self-reliance in this sense is not the issue.

However, like many good things, self-reliance has its own dangerous turn when it becomes the only lens through which a person lives, plans, serves, or even relates to God. That is the slippery part. It becomes dangerous when it crosses the line into spiritual self-sufficiency. It stops being a strength and becomes a silent rebellion when the heart says, 'I can do it; I do not need God for this.' It becomes a snare when man begins to trust more in himself than in the God who made him. It slowly shifts from dependence on God to independence from God. It is subtle, smooth, and yet very costly.

The deception of self-reliance is not that it appears evil, but that it sounds right. A person may wake up each day, read the Bible, attend church, serve in ministry, and still be ruled by self. This kind of self-reliance is challenging to detect because it often hides behind religious clothing. It appears to be dedication, but deep within, it is driven by the idea of personal ability. There is a way the soul can be full of religious activities and still be empty of God. A person can be present in church yet absent in intimacy. A believer can carry a Bible and still not carry God's presence.

In the book of Revelation, the Lord spoke to the church in Laodicea and exposed this deception. The people had said in their hearts, I am rich, and increased with goods, and have need of nothing; and God responded by saying, "And knowest not that thou art wretched, and miserable, and poor, and blind, and naked" (Revelation 3:17). This is what self-reliance looks like in the spirit. It gives a false sense of sufficiency. The person feels equipped, but in reality, they are empty. They claim they have no need, but God sees that they lack everything that truly matters.

The Laodicean church had grown, most likely had structure, numbers, reputation, and influence. But they had lost the intimacy that mattered to God. What they thought was gain was actually loss. That is the danger when ambition replaces intimacy. That is what happens when a person begins to run a ministry like a business, counting achievements but losing sight of its essence. The heart of God is not measured by the size of a church building, or the number of sermons preached. It is measured by the depth of communion with Him.

Some people start their journey with God in deep intimacy. They prayed not to be seen. They served out of love. They wept in secret and fasted to know God. However, along the way, the journey took a shift. The work of God slowly replaced the walk with God. Ministry became a platform, not a pathway. The secret place was replaced by strategic meetings. Tears in the closet were replaced by applause on stage. Before long, the presence of God was no longer the reward; instead, numbers, fame, and recognition took that place. This is how self-reliance creeps into ministry.

It was not that they became worldly in the usual sense, but they became self-driven. They started relying more on what they knew, what they could do, who they could call, and what they had achieved. God became a name in the conversation, rather than the guide on the journey. And soon, everything became mechanical. They no longer prayed because they wanted to hear God; they prayed because it was expected. They no longer fasted because they desired God; they fasted because there was a program to prepare for. That is how self becomes the center.

In Numbers 20, Moses struck the rock instead of speaking to it as God commanded. Water still came out, the people still drank, and the crowd still celebrated. But Moses had moved into self. That simple act of self-dependence and disobedience cost him the Promised Land. God still provided for the people, but the servant of God missed the mark. This illustrates the dangers of replacing divine instruction with personal ability. Just because something works does not mean it is from God. Fruitfulness does not always mean faithfulness.

Over-reliance on self can make the acts of God become idols. A person can become so carried away with the results that they begin to worship the work itself instead of the One who gave it. The altar becomes a stage. The songs become performances. The church becomes a company. And God becomes a background figure. The danger is that people may not notice when this shift happens, but God does.

In many ways, this is the unseen war that many Christians face. The heart wants to prove something. The mind wants to succeed. The flesh wants applause. The soul wants recognition. And while these desires may look noble on the outside, they begin to choke the life of intimacy from within. Even the desire to win souls or plant churches can become an idol if it replaces the pursuit of God Himself. Ministry must not replace fellowship. Results must not replace relationship.

Self-reliance has a sound. It often sounds like: I will do it. I know how to handle this. I got this. It is all about me. I built this ministry. I trained these leaders. I prayed this revival into existence. I preached, and the church grew. That language betrays a hidden confidence in self. That is why James reminded the believers to say, "If the Lord will, we shall live, and do this, or that" (James 4:15). Not because it is wrong to plan, but because it is wrong to forget who truly owns the breath that sustains the planner.

There was a king called Uzziah in 2 Chronicles 26. He started well. God helped him. He built cities. He had a powerful army. He was marvelously helped till he was strong. But when he was strong, his heart was lifted to his destruction. That is the danger. When God enables a person, they must remain small in their own eyes. But Uzziah entered the temple to burn incense, which was only permitted for priests. He felt he could do anything. That act of spiritual self-confidence led to leprosy and shame.

Even Jesus, though He was the Son of God, declared in John 5:19,

"The Son can do nothing of himself, but what he seeth the Father do."

If Jesus could not operate independently of the Father, who then can? This should humble every believer. No amount of growth should lead to self-glorification. No level of impact should remove the need for direction. No success in ministry should take away the need for submission. The more God lifts a person, the more they must depend on Him.

It is not wrong to desire more churches. It is not bad to want more souls saved. It is not wrong to seek revival. But it is wrong when those desires become replacements for time with God. If the strategy meeting takes more attention than the prayer altar, something is wrong. If the sermon preparation becomes more important than the Word of God speaking to the preacher first, then the self is at work. God is not against plans. But He is against pride.

Self-reliance wears many faces. It can look like confidence. It can sound like experience. It can feel like maturity. But if it is not rooted in constant fellowship with God, it is just a mask. It may work for a while. It may even produce some results. But in the long run, it will cost the person what matters most. That is why Jesus would often go to the mountain to pray, even when the crowds were waiting. He chose intimacy over activity. He withdrew from popularity to seek the Father. That was His secret.

Ministry is not proof of closeness to God. Success is not always a sign of God's favor. The real proof is dependence. The sign of genuine relationship with God is not only in what is produced outwardly but in the posture of the heart inwardly. A heart that trembles at His word. A heart that consults God before taking a step. A heart that surrenders even good plans at His feet. That is the cure for self-reliance.

Many believers have fallen into the same trap, especially those with great zeal. Zeal is not enough. Passion is not preservation. A person can burn for God and still burn out, not because the fire has died, but because God no longer maintains it. It became a fire they tried to fan by themselves.

That is how the battle begins. The flesh wants to run, while the Spirit says, "Wait." The mind says act, but God says stay. And if the person is not careful, they begin to see obedience as delay. They start to feel that prayer is slowing them down. They want things to move fast. They want the church to grow. They want the platform to expand. And in that impatience, they begin to take steps God never ordered. Like Abraham with Hagar, they create an Ishmael because waiting for Isaac seemed too long.

Self-reliance is not just a character issue. It is a heart issue. It is about what a person truly believes in their inner man. If they do not believe that God alone can sustain, build, and lead, then they will begin to lean on themselves when pressure increases. Proverbs 3:5 says,

"Trust in the Lord with all thine heart; and lean not unto thine own understanding."

That is not advice. That is a command. Leaning on one's understanding may look like wisdom, but it is foolishness when God is left out.

The more a person grows in spiritual responsibility, the more dangerous self-reliance becomes. That is because experience can deceive. A person may feel they have seen enough, preached enough, prayed enough, and learned enough to now operate by default. That is when the flesh becomes the driver, and the Holy Spirit becomes a passenger. Slowly, the language of dependence fades. There is less asking and more assuming, less waiting and more doing. And slowly, the ministry becomes performance-driven.

This can also be seen in the life of Samson. He was gifted. He was anointed. He was chosen from birth. But along the way, he began to live as though the anointing was his property. He broke the Nazarite vow. He touched what he was not supposed to touch. And finally, in Judges 16, he rose up and said, "I will go out as at other times before, and shake myself." But the Bible says, ". . . he wist not that the Lord was departed from him." That is one of the most tragic verses in the Bible. He did not even know that God had left. He still thought he could operate as before.

This is what happens when a person walks too long in the shadow of self-reliance. They lose awareness of divine absence. They keep working. They keep ministering. But God is no longer involved. They become like a machine that is still running but disconnected from its source. And because results may still be forthcoming, they assume God is still involved. But God is not always in the results. God is in the obedience.

There are churches where the programs are perfect, but the presence is absent. Some ministers are articulate but spiritually dry. Some believers are busy but barren. All because the heart shifted from dependence to ability. When a person begins to rely more on planning than on prayer, more on systems than on the Spirit, more on visibility than on vision, they are entering the zone of self-reliance.

Even David, a man after God's own heart, fell into this trap when he numbered the people, as recorded in 2 Samuel 24. God had not commanded it. David just wanted to know how strong his army was. Perhaps he wanted to measure his capacity. Maybe he wanted to evaluate his power. But God was displeased. He sent judgment upon Israel. That single act of self-reliance cost lives. Even though David was deeply spiritual, he still made the mistake of trusting numbers more than the God of the numbers.

Some find themselves comparing ministries, counting followers, tracking views, and measuring growth. None of these are sins by themselves. But when they become the yardstick for progress, and the heart is no longer humbled before God, self-reliance has entered. When decisions are made based on what looks best instead of what God said, it is self-confidence in disguise. The heart may not say it out loud, but it is thinking, I can do this. I know how this works.

Paul warned the church in Galatia, saying,

"Are ye so foolish? Having begun in the Spirit, are ye now made perfect by the flesh?" (Galatians 3:3)

That question still echoes today. Many begin their journey by relying on God, but then attempt to complete it through fleshly strategies. They start with fasting, but now rely on funding. They used to seek God before taking steps, but now they take steps and then ask God to bless them afterward. They begin to mix faith with formulas.

Sometimes, self-reliance emerges when there is a fear of appearing weak. The person wants to be seen as capable. They do not want to be perceived as helpless. So, they stop asking for help. They pretend everything is under control. Even when they are dry spiritually, they fake fire because the image must be maintained. They give answers to questions they have not asked God. They preach truths they are not living. All because self is now the manager of the ministry.

It takes genuine humility to acknowledge one's weaknesses before God. It takes brokenness to say, "I do not know what to do." It takes intimacy to pause and wait, even when pressure says move. But most importantly, it takes trust to let God lead when the path is not clear. That is what self-reliance cannot do. It always wants clarity, proof, assurance, and control. But faith walks blind when God says go. Faith does not ask for signs. Faith obeys without complete understanding.

Jesus taught this lifestyle. He never took steps on His own. He prayed through the night. He listened to the Father. He waited for direction. He moved at the pace of heaven. And He told His disciples,

I do nothing of myself. That should be the model. That should be the pattern. Not one of activity, but of alignment. Not one of ambition, but of attention to God.

Self-reliance always feels justified. It points to pressure, urgency, and deadlines. But obedience cannot be replaced by effort. What a person does for God cannot replace what they do with God. In fact, the devil sometimes pushes people to do more than God instructed, just to wear them out and shift their gaze. The goal is to keep them so busy that they no longer have time to hear God's voice.

Often, burnout in ministry is not due to the workload being too great. It is because the person is carrying what they were never meant to carry. Jesus said,

"My yoke is easy, and my burden is light" (Matthew 11:30).

So, if the burden becomes too heavy, perhaps the person has taken on a load that God did not intend. That is what self-reliance does. It adds weight to the soul and removes peace from the spirit.

CONFRONTING THE THINGS WE SERVE IN SECRET

"Someone can say they are serving God, but a closer look reveals that what fuels the drive is not a heart for God but a hunger for validation, recognition, or self-worth." - Rev Dr. Nadine Nkulu

This is the part of faith that demands honesty. The heart can pretend for a long time, but not forever. Eventually, what lies beneath the actions begins to show in small cracks. The real issue is not whether the actions look spiritual, but whether the motive behind them is aligned with God. That is why the Bible repeatedly emphasizes the importance of the heart. In Proverbs chapter 4 verse 23, it says,

"Keep thy heart with all diligence; for out of it are the issues of life."

The matters of life are not born in the hands but in the heart.

Many people have made sacrifices that appeared noble on the outside but were born out of ambition. Some pursued ministry not because they were sent but because they wanted to build something to feel important. Others chased spiritual platforms because they were trying to escape the pain of not being seen. It is possible to build a church, plant outreaches, write books, and still not be doing it for God. The outer form may reflect light, but the inner fire may be burning for self.

In Acts chapter 5, Ananias and Sapphira serve as a clear warning. They made an offering, and from the outside, it appeared to be a generous act. But their hearts told a different story. They wanted to appear committed, but they were deceiving themselves. Peter said to Ananias in verse 4,

"Why hast thou conceived this thing in thine heart? thou hast not lied unto men, but unto God."

What they did was not wrong in terms of the act. They sold their property and donated the money to the church. But what made it deadly was the intention behind it. They served the idea of status, not the reality of surrender.

Jesus was never impressed by outward appearances. In Matthew chapter 6, He spoke about those who gave, prayed, and fasted to be seen by men. These were religious actions. Yet Jesus said they had already received their reward. That means the intention was not for God but for visibility. The actions were clean, but the motives were corrupt. That is the danger of secret service to things that are not God. People can walk around looking holy, but inwardly, they are chasing something else.

Some serve their own dreams and call it a vision. Others pursue personal comfort and call it purpose. It is not what is said on the surface that matters, but what the heart truly believes. Jeremiah chapter 17 verse 10 says,

"I the Lord search the heart, I try the reins, even to give every man according to his ways, and according to the fruit of his doings."

God does not just see the deed. He looks at the inner compass that guided that deed.

Sometimes what drives a person in ministry is fear, not love. Fear of being forgotten. Fear of failure. Fear of being ordinary. And so, they run, not towards God, but away from insecurity. The ministry becomes a place to hide their wounded sense of self. In that case, they are serving an idol they built inside. They are still in church. They are still quoting scriptures. But deep inside, there is something else seated on the throne.

This was true of King Saul. In 1 Samuel 15, God gave him explicit instructions through the prophet Samuel. Saul was told to destroy the Amalekites and all that they had. But Saul kept the best sheep and oxen. When Samuel confronted him, Saul claimed that the animals were kept to be sacrificed to the Lord. That sounded spiritual, but it was rebellion. Samuel replied in verse 22,

"Hath the Lord as great delight in burnt offerings and sacrifices, as in obeying the voice of the Lord? Behold, to obey is better than sacrifice, and to hearken than the fat of rams."

Saul tried to cover disobedience with religious language. But God saw the truth.

This is why motives must be confronted. The hardest person to be honest with is oneself. People easily convince themselves that they are doing the right thing. But until they are quiet enough to ask why they are doing it, they may never discover that something else is growing in their heart. Even good things can become dangerous when they are built on the wrong foundation. An idol does not always have to be a golden calf. Sometimes it is a personal ambition that was never submitted to God.

This internal conflict is not rare. It happens more often than most people are willing to admit. A person claims to want to serve God, but in reality, they seek to use God to achieve a goal. They fast not because they want to know God, but because they want Him to open a door for them. They give not from love but from expectation. They attend church not out of hunger but out of habit or social pressure. All of these things look right but feel wrong when examined through the lens of sincerity.

There must be a willingness to examine the altar of the heart. In the Old Testament, God always required a pure altar. The sacrifice had to be placed in the right way. No strange fire was allowed. That shows that God is not desperate for activity. He is interested in the state of the one bringing the offering. In Leviticus chapter 10, Nadab and Abihu offered strange fire before the Lord. Fire came out from the presence of the Lord and devoured them. They were priests. They were sons of Aaron. Yet God did not overlook their action. They introduced what God did not command. Their ministry evolved into a service of self-expression rather than divine instruction.

The same happens today when people serve out of woundedness or ego, when the pulpit becomes a platform for settling personal scores. When the songs are no longer worship but performance. When testimonies are shared not to glorify God but to impress people. When leadership becomes about control rather than servanthood. All these are signs that the heart has shifted. What is done may still carry the name of God, but it no longer holds the approval of heaven.

People need to begin asking honest questions. Why am I really doing this? What am I hoping to gain? Who am I trying to please? What am I afraid of losing? Until these questions are asked, the danger remains hidden. It is possible to pursue success and call it stewardship. It is possible to be obsessed with growth and refer to it as kingdom expansion. But God sees what man cannot see.

The altar of the heart must be cleansed often. Just as in the Old Testament, the priests had to maintain the altar daily. They had to remove ashes and keep the fire burning. That was not a one-time act. It was continuous. Similarly, people today must constantly check their motives. Even good things can turn into pride if the heart is not guarded.

A man can pray for revival but secretly desire to be the one God uses. A woman can serve in church but be silently comparing herself to others. A youth can desire spiritual gifts, but only for attention. All these are forms of secret service to self. They look spiritual on the outside but are selfish on the inside. God does not reward such service. He is not manipulated by actions. He responds to genuine surrender.

Paul said in 1 Corinthians 4:5 that God will bring to light the hidden things of darkness and make the counsels of the hearts manifest. That means even things people hide well will one day be exposed. God will reveal the reason behind every word, every message, every project, and every ministry. The judgment will not be about what was done but why it was done. That is the true test of spiritual service.

DISCUSSION QUESTIONS

1. How can something good like ministry, family, career, or personal dreams quietly become an idol without us realizing it?

2. Jesus said, "Where your treasure is, there your heart will be also." What "treasures" tend to pull your heart's focus away from God the most?

3. In what ways can spiritual activities (praying, serving, preaching, leading) become driven by self-ambition or validation instead of intimacy with God?

4. Inner idol often "feels right." What signs can help us recognize when our desires or goals have begun to replace God at the center?

5. Why do you think self-reliance is such a subtle but dangerous form of idolatry, especially for people who serve or lead in ministry?

6. If God asked you to lay down your biggest dream, desire, or sense of identity—as He asked Abraham to lay down Isaac - what emotions would that surface in you?

7. What practical steps can help you consistently move from self-driven living to God-dependent living in your daily decisions, ministry, and desires?

Chapter Seven

RETURNING TO THE SECRET PLACE

The strength of any army is not only found in its weapons but also in the quality of its secret places."
- Rev. Dr. Nadine Nkulu

Jesus said in Matthew chapter 6:6, "But thou, when thou prayest, enter into thy closet, and when thou hast shut thy door, pray to thy Father which is in secret and thy Father which seeth in secret shall reward thee openly."

In this simple instruction, the picture of the secret place becomes clearer. It is not merely the shutting of a door. It is the shutting out of distractions. It is not only privacy from men, but also a presence with God. It is not only silence but surrender. The Father is in the secret. That is where He sees. That is where He responds.

In the Old Testament, the secret place was not new. Psalm 91:1 declares,

"He that dwelleth in the secret place of the most High shall abide under the shadow of the Almighty."

There is a place where safety is assured not because of walls but because of Who lives there. The secret place is not simply a room. It is not always a location. It is a spiritual positioning. It is the posture of a soul that has shut out everything and has turned fully to God. It is not a formula. It is not a performance. It is a genuine retreat of the heart.

David understood this place deeply. In Psalm 27:5, he wrote,

"For in the time of trouble he shall hide me in his pavilion in the secret of his tabernacle shall he hide me he shall set me up upon a rock."

He not only knew God as a Shepherd or King. He knew God as a hiding place. A place of renewal. A place where his soul could be covered. The secret place was never designed to be a reward. It was always a necessity.

When a person begins drifting away from this place, they may still attend church. They may still quote scripture. They may even still serve in ministry. But something is off. They are not where they used to be. Their voice may still sound loud, but their heart is quiet. Their life may still look active, but their spirit is tired. They know it. God knows it. But sometimes, no one else does. This is how shadows form. When the secret place is no longer sacred, the outside begins to cover the inside.

To return to the secret place is to admit that one has left. It is to recognize that routines have replaced reverence. That schedules have taken over surrender. That the relationship has been reduced to responsibility. It is not just about praying again. It is about longing again. It is not about starting devotion. It is about renewing affection. Many who have walked with God for years sometimes find themselves lost. Not because they turned to sin but because they turned away from presence.

The example of Jacob comes to mind. In Genesis 32, he was about to meet Esau after many years. He had family, wealth, and servants. But that night, he sent everyone away. The Bible says in verse twenty-four,

"And Jacob was left alone and there wrestled a man with him until the breaking of the day."

Alone did not mean abandoned. It meant prepared. That was the secret place. A place of encounter. A place of brokenness. A place of transformation. God did not meet Jacob with a crowd. He met him when he was by himself, when everything else had been set aside.

The journey back to the secret place often begins with an inner discomfort. A knowing that there is more. A sense that something important has been ignored. It is not always marked by significant events. Sometimes it is the still voice amidst activity. Sometimes it is a weariness that rest cannot solve. Sometimes it is a hunger that food cannot fill. It is the voice of the Father calling. Calling not to punish, but to pour again. Calling not to remind of failures, but to restore fellowship.

The secret place strips a person of performance. It reduces them to just one thing. A child before the Father. Not a preacher. Not a singer. Not a leader. Just one soul reaching out to the One who knows. In this place, pride dies. Titles mean nothing. Accolades are silent. Only honesty lives there. Only truth breathes there. It is where people cry, and no one judges. It is where people confess, and heaven listens. It is where grace is poured without explanation. And yet, many avoid it.

Sometimes it is fear. Sometimes it is shame. Sometimes it is the busyness of ministry or life. But whatever the excuse, the result is the same. Emptiness. The outward strength that lacks inward substance. The ability to perform but not to commune. When the secret place is missing, everything else becomes an act. Words lose weight. Worship loses warmth. There is still motion, but no emotion. It is possible to be near the altar but far from the throne.

Scripture does not merely suggest the secret place. It reveals it as a model. Moses often went up the mountain to speak with God. He left the people, the noise, and the demands. Exodus chapter thirty-four verse twenty-eight says,

"And he was there with the Lord forty days and forty nights he did neither eat bread nor drink water. And he wrote upon the tables the words of the covenant, the ten commandments."

It was not only a place of fellowship but of instruction. Moses did not only feel God there. He heard God there. Direction was received. Clarity was restored.

Jesus modeled this lifestyle consistently. In Mark 1:35, it says,

"And in the morning rising up a great while before day he went out and departed into a solitary place and there prayed."

Even the Son of God knew the weight of solitude with the Father. It was not a habit. It was a necessity. He went not just to talk but to be strengthened. Not just to pray but to receive.

In Luke chapter five verse sixteen, it says,

"And he withdrew himself into the wilderness and prayed."

He pulled away. He disconnected. That was the pattern. Before power, there was presence. Before ministry, there was communion. Before signs, there was surrender. The secret place is never public, but its effects are always visible. What is done in secret is revealed in strength. What is poured out in hiddenness shows up in boldness.

Sometimes, men and women return to this place through pain. A loss. A mistake. A season of brokenness. Not all storms are meant to destroy. Some are to awaken. Jonah found himself in the belly of a fish. He cried from there. In Jonah chapter two verse one, it says,

"Then Jonah prayed unto the Lord his God out of the fish's belly."

That was his secret place. A strange one. But a real one. God heard him there. Because God hears from anywhere the heart is true.

Even Jesus, before the cross, found Himself in Gethsemane. A garden. A private place. In Luke 22:44, it says, "And being in an agony he prayed more earnestly and his sweat was as it were great drops of blood falling down to the ground." That was no ordinary moment. That was deep surrender. That was full submission. He was not just fulfilling prophecy. He was showing us the weight of being alone with the Father. The cost. The intimacy. The reality.

Many times, revival begins there. Not on a stage. Not with a mic. But in a room. A corner. A moment. One person on their knees. Not trying to be seen. Not hoping to be heard by men. Just wanting God. Wanting more. And in that moment, heaven moves. Because God always honors the secret place. He always meets the heart that meets Him there.

THE CALL TO INTIMACY OVER ACTIVITY
"The Church must return to the kind of Christianity that prioritizes

the secret place over public platform." - Rev Dr. Nadine Nkulu

Those who heard the call and responded became men and women of depth. Their lives were not driven by outward applause but by inward assurance. They knew something others only imagined. They had touched something sacred. They had heard the whisper behind the noise. And that changed everything. When Elijah ran from Jezebel in First Kings chapter nineteen, he ended up in a cave. Tired. Afraid. Frustrated. But it was there that God called him. Not through the wind. Not through the earthquake. Not through the fire. But through a still small voice. That voice did not call him back to the crowds. It called him back to communion. It did not demand activity. It invited alignment.

This is the same voice many ignore today. The voice that says, Stop striving. Come closer. Lay it all down. Just listen. That voice is gentle but firm. It does not scream, but it never stays silent. It is the voice that values presence over performance. It reminds the soul that God wants the heart more than the hustle. And until that call is answered, fulfillment will remain out of reach.

The greatest deception is not found in outright rebellion. It is found in distracted devotion. When the enemy cannot stop a person, he will try to speed them up. He will fill their days with so much noise that they cannot hear the whisper. He will make them efficient but empty. Productive but powerless. Busy but broken. That is why the call to intimacy is urgent. It is a rescue. It is a mercy. It is God saying, Before you lose yourself in what you are doing, find Me again.

David understood this call. He was a king, a warrior, a poet, and a leader. But he was first a lover of God. In Psalm 27:4, he said,

"One thing have I desired of the Lord, that will I seek after. That I may dwell in the house of the Lord all the days of my life, to behold the beauty of the Lord and to inquire in His temple."

That was intimacy. That was desire. That was the voice of a man who knew that crowns mean nothing if presence is lost.

When God called Jeremiah, He did not begin with tasks. He started with touch. Jeremiah 1:9 says,

"Then the Lord put forth His hand and touched my mouth. And

the Lord said unto me, Behold, I have put my words in thy mouth."

That was intimacy. That was encounter. That was not a job. That was a journey. And from that point, Jeremiah spoke as one who knew God. Not just about God.

Activity is easy to measure. It has numbers. It has reports. It has applause. But intimacy is hidden. It has no spotlight. It has no certificate. But it has weight. It carries something the world cannot copy. That is why God calls men to it. Because He knows that only intimacy can carry the kind of glory that does not destroy. He knows that without nearness, usefulness becomes dangerous. That is why He draws men back. Not to punish. But to purify.

Those who have walked this path often describe it with deep emotion. They remember what it felt like to wake up and know God was near. They remember the tears that came without music. The insights that came without study. The strength that came without striving. And they know that no stage, no salary, no strategy can replace that place. That place where the soul meets the Spirit. That place where God is not a subject but a Person.

In *The Pursuit of God*, Tozer wrote, "God waits to be wanted." That is a powerful line. It reveals the patience of God. The humility of God. That He does not force. He invites. He waits. And when a person answers that call, everything changes. Not always outwardly. But inwardly. The noise becomes clearer. The questions become quieter. The heart becomes softer. That is the fruit of intimacy.

There is a kind of boldness that does not come from knowledge. It comes from nearness. The apostles in Acts chapter four were described as unlearned and ignorant men, yet they spoke with such authority that even the council was amazed. Verse thirteen says,

"They took knowledge of them, that they had been with Jesus."

That was the difference. Not grammar. Not degrees. Presence. That was what gave their words weight.

The Church must return to this. It must return to the kind of Christianity that prioritizes the secret place over public platform. Those values being known by God more than being known by men. That listens more than it speaks. That worships more than it works. That stays more than it moves. That kind of life may look slow to others, but it produces something eternal.

Every revival that lasted began with intimacy. It started with men and women who were not in a hurry. Who stayed with God until He moved. Who wept before they preached. Who listened before they led. That was the secret. Not systems. Not skill. But surrender. And that surrender began with a call. A call to leave the noise. To leave the crowd. To leave the performance. And to return. Return to the place where the fire first fell. Return to the place where God was not an assignment but a friend.

CULTIVATING STILLNESS IN A NOISY WORLD

"Before there is realignment, there must be seasons of stillness. Not to make one less useful but to make one more aligned." - Rev Dr. Nadine Nkulu

The Bible reveals that God often prepares men through stillness. It is not always the spectacular that marks divine seasons. Sometimes it is the quiet, the pause, the stop. Before Moses became the deliverer of Israel, he was pulled into forty years of stillness. In Exodus chapter three, he was tending sheep. That was far from the palace he had grown up in. It was not a season of activity. It was a season of quiet. But it was there, in that stillness, that he saw the burning bush. It was there that he heard the voice of God. The calling did not come in Pharaoh's court. It came in a silent place. A place where ego had been emptied. A place where pride had been stripped.

Stillness was never about laziness. It was about preparation. It was about alignment. It was about the emptying that makes room for filling. Many people want God to speak in the fire, but they do not know He also speaks in the fold. In the ordinary. In the waiting. When Joseph was thrown into prison after being sold into slavery and falsely accused, it was not just injustice. It was stillness. It was silence. That prison became a womb for discernment. It was there that Joseph learned to interpret dreams. Not just as a skill but as a responsibility. And when the time came, he stood before Pharaoh, not just as a free man but as a prepared man. The stillness had not broken him. It had built him.

In Psalm 46:10, the scripture says,

"Be still, and know that I am God."

This was not a suggestion. It was a command. The knowing of God is tied to the stillness of man. A man who cannot be still cannot know God deeply. Because the nature of God is not always loud, his leading is not always in flashes. Sometimes it is in whispers. Sometimes it is in waiting. That knowing cannot be replaced by sermons or songs. It comes from stillness.

There are moments when God will deliberately shut the doors to activity. Not as punishment. But as preservation. He is not in a hurry, unlike men. He is not impressed by schedules. Platforms do not move Him. What He seeks is a heart. And sometimes, to find that heart, He must interrupt the noise. He must pull back the curtain. He must call men away. Away from doing. Away from proving. Into being. Into knowing.

In today's world, stillness is often uncomfortable. People are trained to move fast. To respond quickly. To achieve constantly. But God does not work on human timelines. When He wanted to teach Israel dependence, He gave them manna daily. Not weekly. Not monthly. That daily provision required daily stillness. They had to stop, wait, receive, and rest. It was a spiritual lesson wrapped in a natural routine.

The kind of stillness that brings true intimacy is not idle. It is intentional. It means shutting the world out to open the heart up. It means turning off the external noise so that the internal voice of God can be heard. It means sitting with the Word, not for teaching but for transformation. It means praying not to be heard but to hear. This kind of stillness is active. It is full of attention. It listens more than it speaks. It surrenders more than it seeks.

This stillness is where intimacy is born. Because it forces one to face what activity often hides. In stillness, the motives are exposed. The fears are confronted. The desires are refined. It is in this quietness that God speaks not just to circumstances but to identity. He reminds the heart of who it is. Whose it is. And what truly matters.

Some people have come to know God deeply not through preaching but through pain. Pain often introduces stillness. It halts what movement once covered. In that quietness, they learned to see

God. To trust Him. To lean into Him. Job said in Job 42:5,

"I have heard of thee by the hearing of the ear, but now mine eye seeth thee."

That was the fruit of stillness. Not silence alone, but surrender.

The season of stillness in a person's life may not come with applause. It may not bring increase. It may even look like loss. But in the Kingdom, loss often precedes gain. Jesus said in John 12:24,

"Except a corn of wheat fall into the ground and die, it abideth alone. But if it die, it bringeth forth much fruit."

That is the pattern. Stillness. Death to the flesh. Then life in the Spirit.

What should be done in such seasons? First, listen, not with the ears but with the heart. Stillness invites discernment. In that place, the Lord often gives clarity that noise had hidden. Second, wait. Do not rush what God is still shaping. Impatience aborts the process. Third, trust. Even when nothing seems to be changing, trust that something is being built. Character. Patience. Depth. These are not visible at first. But they will show later.

In *The Knowledge of the Holy*, Tozer wrote, "It is doubtful whether God can bless a man greatly until He has hurt him deeply." That hurt is not always punishment. Sometimes it is stillness. God making space in a man before He adds substance. That space is sacred. It is not empty. It is expectant. It waits not just for activity to resume but for alignment to take place. In times of stillness, the Word becomes more alive. Scriptures that were once skimmed now speak clearly. Prayer becomes deeper. Worship becomes honest. It is in stillness that the soul finds healing. Not from noise, but from the ache of distance. Because when one has lived too long away from God, stillness becomes the road back.

The heart that longs for God must learn to sit with Him. Not rush Him. Not use Him. Just know Him. And that knowing comes not from doing more, but from being still. David said in Psalm 62:5,

"My soul, wait thou only upon God, for my expectation is from Him."

That was not a man chasing answers. That was a man anchored in stillness.

There are no shortcuts to this. One cannot borrow stillness. It must be embraced. It must be chosen. The world may call it wasted time. But heaven calls it worship. Because in that place, God speaks. And when He speaks, everything realigns.

It is in the seasons of stillness that the heart returns to what truly matters. The world trains people to be noticed, but God trains them to be known. And to be known by God, one must come to Him as a child. Not in performance. But in posture. In stillness, pride loses its place. Achievements become silent. Titles fall away. It is just the soul and the Maker.

Stillness also helps in healing what busyness concealed. Some people are wounded but active. They keep moving to avoid the pain. They continue to work to avoid silence. But God will not ignore what they buried. He will bring them into a season where they must sit with their hearts. Not to harm them. But to heal them. That healing is part of intimacy. It cannot happen when people are always running. It happens when they stop.

The kind of stillness that changes a person is not external only. It must enter the inner life. The thoughts. The beliefs. The imagination. That is where God speaks deeply. He says,

"Come now, and let us reason together, saith the Lord."

That invitation is not for the busy. It is for the still. For the ones who can stop long enough to listen.

Even nature teaches the value of stillness. A seed does not grow when it is moved every day. It must be still. It must stay buried. It must wait. Then, in due season, it breaks forth. That is also the secret of spiritual growth. Many want to grow fast. But God is not in a hurry. He is not after quantity. He is after quality.

Stillness does not mean inactivity. It means undistracted attention. It means being present with God, as Mary was in Luke 10. She sat at Jesus' feet. She listened. She was still. Martha was busy. She was moving. She was serving. But she missed the better part. Jesus said, Mary hath chosen that good part, which shall not be taken away from her.

Those who choose stillness will often be misunderstood. People may call them unproductive. However, what they are gaining in intimacy cannot be seen at first glance. It will show later. It will reflect in peace. In wisdom. In obedience. Because time with God is never wasted.

Stillness is not weakness. It is strength under control. It is the posture of those who know that God is worth waiting for. Isaiah chapter thirty verse fifteen says, In quietness and in confidence shall be your strength. That is the power of stillness. It gives strength that activity cannot.

And when the season of stillness ends, the fruit is unmistakable. Moses returned with clarity. Joseph emerged with authority. Jesus came out of the wilderness in power. Because stillness does not just quiet the heart. It equips the soul.

DISCUSSION QUESTIONS

1. When you hear the phrase "secret place," what comes to your mind personally? A room? A feeling? A season?

2. What makes it hardest for you to shut out distractions—your schedule, your phone, your thoughts, or something else?

3. Have you ever gone through a season where you were active in church but empty inside? What helped you notice it?

4. What usually alerts you that you've drifted from intimacy with God—even if your life still looks "spiritual" on the outside?

5. Why do you think God meets people so powerfully in quiet places—like Jacob alone, Moses on the mountain, or Jesus in the wilderness?

6. What does stillness with God look like for you in real life—not the ideal, but the practical?

7. Can you remember a moment when God used stillness, pain, or discomfort to pull you back to Him? What changed afterward?

8. What is one small, realistic step you can take this week to make space for the secret place again?

Chapter Eight

REDISCOVERING GOD'S VOICE

G od desired intimacy, but man preferred a middleman. That middleman culture still exists today."
- Rev. Dr. Nadine Nkulu

In Psalm 29:3 it is written that, "The voice of the Lord is upon the waters: the God of glory thundereth: the Lord is upon many waters." That statement is not an exaggeration. It is the reality of how weighty the voice of God is. Verse four continues to describe the voice of the Lord as powerful and full of majesty. Then the following verses speak of how the voice of the Lord "breaketh the cedars and divideth the flames of fire." "It shaketh the wilderness and makes the hinds to calve." This is not a still whisper. This is thunder that carries divine force. This thunder is not to cause fear but to arrest the heart of man. It is a sound that should make a man pause and think. When thunder rumbles, most people freeze or instinctively bow their heads. It is as though nature itself bows to the voice of the

Creator.

In John 12:28, Jesus lifted a prayer saying, "Father glorify thy name and then came there a voice from heaven saying I have both glorified it and will glorify it again." Then in verse 29, it was recorded that the people who stood by and heard it said that it thundered; others said an angel spoke to him. This shows that the voice of God can thunder, but even then, men may not understand it. Some only heard noise. Some thought it was an angel. Yet the Son heard the Father clearly. This is where the real concern lies. If the voice of God is powerful enough to sound like thunder and yet men cannot discern it, then there is a deeper problem. It is not with the voice. It is with the ears of men.

To rediscover the voice of God, one must begin by accepting that God has always been speaking. He is not silent. He never stopped. What changed is the posture of man. Sin dulled his ears. Distraction robbed him of stillness. Ambition led him to pursue what seemed godly, but not what God was actually saying. The voice of God cannot compete with the noise of human ambition.

The rediscovery of God's voice requires man to remove the filters he has placed on what he thinks God should sound like. God is not obligated to speak through spectacular means. He spoke to Moses through a bush. He spoke to Balaam through a donkey. He spoke to Samuel as a child when he had not yet known the voice of the Lord. He spoke to Ezekiel by the river. He spoke to Peter through a vision of unclean animals. He spoke to Paul with a light from heaven. These were different expressions but the same voice. That voice cannot be boxed. It cannot be automated or reduced to a formula. That is why men must be humble in how they seek Him.

Sometimes what people call confusion is simply unfamiliarity with how God now chooses to speak. God spoke once in thunder and lightning at Mount Sinai, and the people begged that He should not speak directly to them again. They told Moses to be the one to speak to them instead. That distance created a system where the voice of God was no longer direct. God desired intimacy, but man preferred a middleman. That middleman culture still exists today. People prefer that others hear God on their behalf. But that is not how God designed it. The veil has been torn. Access has been granted. It is now the responsibility of every believer to tune their ears to that voice.

In the book of Hebrews, chapter 3:15, it is said

"Today if ye will hear his voice harden not your hearts."

The voice of God often meets resistance, not because it is unclear, but because the heart of man is already decided. Rediscovering the voice of God means letting go of pre-determined paths. It means taking time to sit with the Word. The written Word of God is one of the purest forms of His voice. It is the voice of God captured in letters. If a believer does not know what God has said in scripture, they will struggle to discern what He is saying in the spirit.

There are times when believers pray for direction, and it seems like God is silent. But the silence is not absence. It is often a pause that invites the believer to search. In Proverbs, chapter 25:2, it says

"It is the glory of God to conceal a thing, but the honour of kings is to search out a matter."

This searching is not intellectual alone. It is spiritual hunger. It is asking like Samuel did, "Speak Lord, for thy servant heareth." It is waking up in the night when sleep is heavy because the spirit senses a stirring. It is turning off the phone not just to fast from food but from noise. The voice of God is not lost. It is simply waiting for men who will wait on it.

God's voice can also be rediscovered through obedience. Sometimes the voice seems silent because the last instruction was not followed. When Saul lost the kingdom, it was not because he did not hear God. It was because he heard and did not obey. Disobedience muffles the voice over time. The more a man disobeys, the more he assumes God has stopped speaking. But He has not. He is waiting for the heart to return. In Isaiah chapter 30:21, it says

"And thine ears shall hear a word behind thee saying, 'This is the way, walk ye in it when ye turn to the right hand and when ye turn to the left.'"

That inner prompting is real. But it comes alive when the heart is surrendered.

Rediscovering God's voice is not a seasonal project. It is a lifelong posture. It is asking God to tune the inner man. It is recognizing that sometimes His voice may lead through valleys, not just mountains. Through silence, not just sermons. Through rebuke, not just comfort. Through discipline, not just prophecy. And throughout Scripture, this is how He dealt with men. When Adam sinned, the voice still came walking in the garden in the cool of the day. When Jonah fled, the word of the Lord came unto Jonah the second time. When Peter denied Him, Jesus still found him after the resurrection and said, "Lovest thou me more than these?" That is the mercy of God's voice. It comes again and again. It thunders, but it also whispers. It breaks, but it also binds. It calls, but it also waits. That voice is not distant. It is near. And every man who truly desires it must first quieten the world within. Only then can the thunder make sense and the whisper become clear.

HEARING AGAIN AMID THE CHAOS

"When a person walks with another consistently, they begin to understand them deeply. Even a glance or a simple tone can communicate volumes. The same applies in the walk with God." - Rev Dr. Nadine Nkulu

When a person is close to someone, they do not need to yell to be heard. They can whisper. And the whisper still makes perfect sense. The same applies to the voice of God. When a person is in true relationship with God, they begin to hear Him differently. The chaotic noise around does not cancel the still small voice. Instead, that voice cuts through everything because it is not a noise; it is a knowing. It is not a sound always heard with the ears; it is a presence felt in the heart.

Elijah learned this lesson in a cave, far from the mountaintop experience he once had. He had seen fire fall from heaven. He had watched rain return at his word. He had outrun the king's chariot by divine strength. However, in 1 Kings 19, when his soul was overwhelmed and chaos reigned within, he discovered another side of God. The Lord passed by, and a great and strong wind tore the mountains and broke the rocks in pieces. But the Lord was not in the wind. After the wind, there was an earthquake, but the Lord was not in the earthquake. After the earthquake came fire, but the Lord was not in the fire. Then came a still small voice. And that was where the Lord was.

The prophet was used to thunder and display. But in his moment of exhaustion, God did not thunder. He whispered. This was not weakness. This was intimacy. The chaos outside was nothing compared to the noise within. Elijah was afraid, alone, disappointed, and confused. He did not need more noise. He needed clarity. He needed presence. That is what God gave him in the still small voice.

The same voice that guided Elijah still speaks today. But many cannot hear it because they are expecting it to thunder. They believe God only speaks when there is shaking, or when a prophetic fire is present, or when someone else confirms what they already feel. But sometimes, God speaks in the quiet thoughts, in the scriptures read alone. In the moment of reflection while walking, in the whisper of correction when about to make a wrong decision.

Chaos is a reality of life. There is noise from within and from outside. There is pressure from the world, confusion from people, and distraction from oneself. Hearing God again in the midst of this chaos is not about shouting louder prayers or doing more religious acts. It is about finding stillness within. It is about cultivating intimacy. It is spiritual sensitivity. It is not laziness. It is attention. Stillness creates room for reception. If a person is always talking, they will never hear. If their mind is always racing, they will miss what is being said. This is why the discipline of quietness is essential for every believer who desires to hear again amid the chaos.

One must understand that chaos will not always end before the voice comes. Sometimes, the voice comes in the middle of the storm. When Jesus walked on water toward His disciples in Matthew 14, a storm was raging. The winds were contrary. The disciples were afraid. But in the midst of that, Jesus spoke, saying,

"Be of good cheer; it is I; be not afraid."

The voice came in the chaos, not after it.

The expectation that everything must calm down before God speaks is not always accurate. God is not limited by noise. But man is. So, the key is not to wait for the storm to stop. The key is to still the heart in the middle of it. God can speak through a verse of scripture, through a gentle conviction, through a burden to pray, or through an uncommon peace about a situation that makes no sense naturally.

Scripture proves that the voice of God is not always dramatic. In Genesis 3:8, the Bible says,

"And they heard the voice of the Lord God walking in the garden in the cool of the day."

That is not thunder. That is companionship. That is relational. Adam and Eve heard the voice of God, not because they had just fasted or because something powerful had happened. They heard because He was walking with them. That was the normal pattern before the fall.

To return to that pattern, a believer must seek to walk with God daily. When a person walks with another consistently, they begin to understand them deeply. Even a glance or a simple tone can communicate volumes. The same applies in the walk with God. Consistency in devotion, scripture meditation, and worship creates a heart environment where His whisper is enough.

Practical steps to hear God again amid chaos must start with internal quietness. That means dealing with internal conflict, emotional weight, and spiritual dryness. The heart must be at rest. Hebrews 4:11 says,

"Let us labour therefore to enter into that rest."

It sounds like a contradiction to labor for rest, but it is not. Rest is not the absence of activity. It is the presence of trust. Trust silences fear. Trust removes noise.

Sometimes, it is not sin that blocks the voice. It is fear. It is anxiety. It is a mind that is too busy to be taught. It is a heart that is too restless to recognize Him.

David said in Psalm 62:5,

"My soul, wait thou only upon God; for my expectation is from him."

This was a man who understood inner stillness. He learned to calm his soul so that his spirit could hear. When expectations shift to God alone, other voices lose their influence. That is when the still small voice becomes clear again.

Scriptural experiences also point to the reality that God speaks more clearly in stillness. In Habakkuk 2:1, the prophet said,

"I will stand upon my watch, and set me upon the tower, and will watch to see what he will say unto me."

Watching to see what God will say sounds unusual, but it makes sense spiritually. The eyes and ears of the spirit are connected. What a person focuses on influences what they hear.

In Acts 10, when Peter was hungry and went up to pray, he fell into a trance and saw a vision. God spoke through that experience. But it happened because he took time apart to seek. He was not distracted. The voice came with clarity. It was not thunder. It was instruction.

Job, in all his affliction and questions, came to a place where he said in Job 42:5,

"I have heard of thee by the hearing of the ear: but now mine eye seeth thee."

There was a shift from hearing about God to knowing Him personally. That shift happened amid suffering, but it brought clarity.

When the heart is stripped of distractions, then the voice becomes distinct. It is not always a dramatic message. Sometimes it is just a reassurance. Sometimes it is a new hunger for scripture. At other times, it is a sudden insight while doing something ordinary. But it always aligns with the nature of God and the truth of His word.

In the book, *Experiencing God*, by Henry Blackaby, he wrote, "God speaks by the Holy Spirit through the Bible, prayer, circumstances, and the church to reveal Himself, His purposes, and His ways." That means one must remain open to these channels, especially in times of chaos. The voice may not come in one predictable form. It is often revealed through multiple confirmations.

To hear again amid chaos is not about trying to control the chaos. It is about tuning the heart. When a radio is off-frequency, it cannot receive the signal even if the station is broadcasting. The same principle applies. The Spirit of God is always speaking, but the soul must be tuned through quietness, attention, and expectancy.

The book *Whisper* by Mark Batterson speaks to this idea. He said, "The voice of God is the key to discovering your destiny and fulfilling your potential." That voice is not always loud. Often, it is subtle. But it is enough.

This truth must be rediscovered by those who feel lost in the shadows. The chaos will not always end. But in the midst of it, God still speaks. And His sheep still know His voice. John 10:27 says,

"My sheep hear my voice, and I know them, and they follow me."

But the danger many face is not that God is no longer speaking; it is that they have grown dull of hearing. Hebrews 5:11 says,

"Of whom we have many things to say, and hard to be uttered, seeing ye are dull of hearing."

That dullness is not about volume. It is about spiritual sensitivity. When the heart becomes weighed down with cares, worries, or offense, it creates spiritual noise that muffles the voice of God.

RECOGNIZING GOD IN THE ORDINARY

"The ability to recognize Him in the ordinary is a direct result of deep fellowship." - Rev Dr. Nadine Nkulu

It was Kenneth Hagin who once wrote that if the Holy Ghost wore a red face cap and red or black clothing, some believers would still not recognize Him. That statement was not just to criticize spiritual blindness, but to confront a major issue: many people have become trained to expect God only in dramatic terms. They wait for thunder, earthquakes, fire from heaven, or a loud voice echoing through the atmosphere before they can say God is speaking or God is present. But one of the most consistent patterns in Scripture and in life is that God often moves through the ordinary.

It is intimacy that helps a person recognize God in such ways. A person who does not know someone deeply can only identify them by their loudness, clothing, or environment. But those who are close, who live with someone, can sense their presence even in silence. That is how it is with God. The ability to recognize Him in the ordinary is a direct result of deep fellowship. Without that closeness, people walk with Him and still miss Him.

After Jesus rose from the dead, He appeared to two of His followers on the road to Emmaus, as recorded in Luke 24. They walked with Him. He spoke with them. He even explained scripture to them. But they did not recognize Him. They only saw a traveler. It was not until He broke the bread that their eyes were opened. He had done something ordinary. He had broken bread. That action was enough for them to know it was Him. Why? Because they had seen Him break bread before. Their memory of intimacy brought recognition.

That story shows that Jesus did not raise His voice or glow with glory on that road. He used conversation. He used scripture. He used bread. Those were ordinary things. But within those ordinary things was the presence of the extraordinary. That is the way God moves. And unless a person trains their heart through fellowship, they will continue to miss Him when He comes without thunder.

Sometimes, God walks into a room through the smile of a child. Sometimes He enters through a question someone asks at the right moment. At other times, He passes by through a gentle reminder in the heart or through a thought that refuses to go away. It may come while sweeping the house or walking down the street. These are ordinary moments. But to the spiritually sensitive, they become holy encounters.

The way of God is not always loud. When He came in the flesh, He was born in a manger. He did not grow up in a palace. He did not wear gold crowns. He did not announce Himself with fanfare. Isaiah 53 described Him by saying,

"He hath no form nor comeliness; and when we shall see him, there is no beauty that we should desire him."

He came through a carpenter's house. He walked dusty roads. He sat with fishermen and tax collectors. Many rejected Him because they expected the Messiah to come in grand style. But God wrapped salvation in the cloth of simplicity. And they missed Him.

In John chapter 4, Jesus met a woman at the well. She had no idea who He was. He did not come with lightning. He simply asked for water. That request turned into a conversation. That conversation turned into a revelation. But it started with thirst. Something as human as being thirsty was the gateway to transformation. If that woman had only looked for the unusual, she would have walked away thinking Jesus was just another man.

This is one of the reasons why intimacy is essential. Intimacy provides insight into a person's patterns. The closer someone is to a person, the more they begin to know how they think, how they act, and what they might say. That same principle applies with God. The closer one is, the easier it is to recognize when He is moving, even if it is in an unexpected way.

Moses understood this concept. In Exodus 33, he said to God, "If thy presence go not with me, carry us not up hence."

That was not a man looking for fireworks. That was someone who had come to value the presence of God so deeply that he did not want to go anywhere without it, whether it looked ordinary or not. Moses had seen the burning bush. He had seen the plagues. He had seen the Red Sea part. But by this point, he was no longer impressed by signs alone. He wanted the presence, even in the quiet.

In the same way, many today have become so trained to associate God only with the loud that they miss Him in the silence. They think God is not speaking because the dream is not dramatic. They believe God is not leading because there was no voice from heaven. But that is not always how He leads. Psalm 32:8 says,

"I will instruct thee and teach thee in the way which thou shalt go: I will guide thee with mine eye."

That means God can guide without saying a word. He can lead through impressions. Through peace. Through unease. Through closed doors. Through the inner knowing.

It is only those who are intimate with God who can tell when that inner knowing is divine. Just as in real life, a mother can sense when her child is not feeling well, even without words being spoken. That is the fruit of closeness. It is not about guessing. It is about understanding. The more a person walks with God, the more they know how He communicates. And often, it is through ordinary situations.

A person may be considering taking a new job. There may be no voice saying go or do not go. But there may be unrest in the heart. Or a strange lack of peace. Or repeated delay. To those who know God well, these are signs. Not dramatic. But clear. Another person may get an idea while listening to a song or watching a scene play out. It may feel natural, but deep inside, it has weight. That is how God speaks sometimes. But if the person is only trained to hear in visions or prophecies, they may miss that moment.

In the book *The Spiritual Man* by Watchman Nee, he explains that spiritual things are not always emotional. He teaches that God often moves in the human spirit, not in the emotions or the intellect. That is why a person may not feel anything dramatic, yet their spirit is deeply aware. That awareness may come in a calm moment, a quiet morning, or while going about a daily task. That is God in the ordinary.

Even in the miracles of Jesus, many things were done through simple acts. He told the man with the withered hand to stretch out his hand. He put mud in the eyes of a blind man and told him to wash it off. He asked people what they had, and they brought loaves and fish. The actions were natural. The power was hidden inside the obedience. But only those who looked beyond the surface could see the divinity inside the simplicity.

There are times when a message in church speaks directly to someone's private question. That message may not come with shouting or a special prophetic declaration. It may be in a single sentence that passes by quickly. But to the sensitive listener, that sentence carries fire. It becomes a word in season. Proverbs 25:11 says,

"A word fitly spoken is like apples of gold in pictures of silver."

That word may look ordinary, but it carries value.

And this is where many lose their way. They believe the absence of drama indicates a lack of God. However, the truth is that many of the loudest experiences are not always the deepest. Some people have had visions and still backslid. Others had dreams and ignored them. However, those who remained sensitive in their walk, those who took the time to recognize God in their daily lives, are the ones who continued to grow.

It is often in washing dishes, walking to work, or riding in traffic that some of the clearest impressions come. That is not a mistake. It is a pattern. God moves through the common. He walks through the mundane. The key is not to search for drama. The key is to remain aware. To live in such a way that even silence becomes sacred.

Even in pain, this truth holds. When Paul asked the Lord to take away the thorn in his flesh, the answer came in a sentence:

"My grace is sufficient for thee."

That was not a show. It was a statement. But it carried weight. Paul said,

"Most gladly therefore will I rather glory in my infirmities."

That shows he heard God through the pain. Through the weakness. Through the ordinary.

Paul did not receive a thunderclap. He received a truth wrapped in a sentence. That is how the Lord speaks at times. He speaks within thoughts. He speaks within moments. He speaks within waiting. But without intimacy, such moments pass unnoticed. People go back to begging for signs, hoping for fire, and searching for what was never promised.

Sometimes God shows up in the neighbor who knocks on the door just in time. Other times He shows up in the courage to forgive someone you thought you could never forgive. That shift in the heart is Him moving. It is not loud. But it is Him. The Holy Ghost does not always wear a red face cap or colored robes. He may wear the voice of a teacher. Or the embrace of a friend. Or the memory of a verse from childhood. But He is still the same Spirit.

DISCUSSION QUESTIONS

1.   Why do you think people today still prefer someone else—like a pastor, prophet, or "spiritual person" to pray for them instead of themselves talking to God directly?

2.   If God's voice is powerful enough to thunder, why do you think so many still struggle to recognize it? What gets in the way?

3.   In your own life, what usually dulls your spiritual ears—sin, busyness, distraction, fear, or something else?

4.   The Bible shows God speaking in many different ways. Which way do you personally find easiest to recognize—and which way is hardest?

5.   Have you ever mistaken God's voice for "noise," like the crowd in John 12? What helped you later realize it was God?

6.   What practical steps help you quiet the noise and tune your heart to hear God again?

7.   Why do you think God values intimacy so deeply and what would change in your walk with Him if you trusted that He truly wants to speak to you directly?

Chapter Nine

LIVING A FULFILLED HEART

L iving a fulfilled heart frees a person from world pressure."
- Rev. Dr. Nadine Nkulu

Living a fulfilled heart means beginning each day without the pressure of needing something external to feel complete. It means waking up with a kind of inward strength that does not depend on what is happening around. A person who lives a fulfilled heart is not desperate for the approval of others or the next big breakthrough. Instead, they draw from a well that runs deep inside, a well dug in secret places with God.

This is not always the case for most people. Many people start their day empty. They wake up chasing things. They look for validation from how others treat them. They expect the world to fill the gap in their soul. And when that does not happen, they feel discouraged. They become restless and frustrated. But a fulfilled heart begins full. Not because everything is perfect, but because it has already found something greater than circumstances.

The Shunammite woman in 2 Kings chapter 4 gives a powerful example. Elisha asked if there was anything she wanted him to do for her. He was ready to speak to the king on her behalf. Yet she responded, "I dwell among mine own people." That response was not casual. It was contentment. She had learned how to rest in her space. She did not live from a place of need. Her fulfillment was not tied to political favor, social status, or miracles. Her heart was settled.

This is different from how many believers live today. Even in church circles, people sometimes chase the spectacular. They do not feel seen unless something grand happens. They measure the presence of God by how loud the atmosphere is. They rate the quality of their walk with God based on answered prayers, visible results, or prophetic affirmations. But none of these are the true measure of a fulfilled heart. Real fulfillment comes before results. It is born in stillness, in trust, in the quiet knowing that God is enough.

When Jesus sat at the well in John chapter 4 and met the Samaritan woman, He made a statement that carried deep meaning. He said,

"Whosoever drinketh of this water shall thirst again: But whosoever drinketh of the water that I shall give him shall never thirst."

What He offered was internal. It was not the removal of physical problems, but the giving of an eternal solution. The water He referred to was spiritual. It would make the receiver complete from within.

The fulfilled heart does not ask, "What next?" every time something is achieved. It is not desperate. It is stable. The Israelites in Numbers 11 received manna that fell from heaven. They had God's presence in the form of a cloud and fire. But they said,

"But now our soul is dried away: there is nothing at all, beside this manna, before our eyes."

They called the provision of God nothing. That is what an unfulfilled heart does. It downplays what God has done and magnifies what it thinks is missing.

That complaint did not start with the food. It began in their soul. When the soul is dry, no blessing can quench its thirst. There will always be something else to crave. The heart will always desire what is not present, ignoring what is already given. Even the supernatural becomes boring to an empty heart. They had manna from heaven, but it was not enough. Why? They had not been trained to live fully from within.

Living with a fulfilled heart is not a sign of laziness. It is not passiveness. It is rest. It is the posture of a soul that has found its anchor. David said in Psalm 23, "The Lord is my shepherd; I shall not want."

That was not a statement of external abundance. That was a declaration of internal sufficiency. Because God was his shepherd, David saw no reason to be in want. That mindset shaped how he saw life.

Many times, people believe that fulfillment will come after something happens. After the promotion. After marriage. After healing. After the testimony. But that is not how God works. He trains His people to live full before the breakthrough. That is why Paul could say in Philippians 4,

"I have learned, in whatsoever state I am, therewith to be content."

He did not say he enjoyed lack. But he learned how to live above it. His heart had been schooled to depend on God, not things.

Living from a fulfilled heart also frees a person from the pressure to prove something. Many people today are trapped in the cycle of performance. They want to be noticed. They want to be admired. They work hard not only to succeed but to be seen succeeding. But when the heart is full, it stops looking for applause. It no longer lives for recognition. It serves. It builds. It gives. All without the hunger to be noticed.

Even in ministry, this is important. A minister who is not full will preach from pressure. They will look for reactions. They will measure success by how people respond. But when the heart is full, the focus shifts. It becomes about obedience, not outcome. Jesus knew who He was. That is why He could wash feet. That is why He could eat with sinners without feeling less. That is why He could stand silent before Pilate. Fulfillment gave Him calmness.

Real fulfillment shows up in small moments. It shows up when someone forgives without needing to be begged. It appears when one gives secretly without seeking praise. It appears when a person chooses peace over winning an argument. These are the fruits of a full heart. They do not scream. But they are strong.

Living from a fulfilled heart means emotions no longer run life. Feelings come and go. Situations rise and fall. But the heart remains steady. Not because everything is predictable, but because the center is fixed.

There is something powerful about living from this place. It silences anxiety. It removes envy. It ends competition. A fulfilled heart does not compare journeys. It celebrates others without feeling smaller. It waits without frustration. It gives without counting because it has found a better treasure.

In Matthew 6, Jesus said,

"But seek ye first the kingdom of God, and his righteousness; and all these things shall be added unto you."

The promise was not just in the adding. It was in the seeking. The one who seeks the kingdom first becomes full by default. And when things are added, they do not become idols. They become tools.

This is why it is dangerous to enter marriage, ministry, or even leadership with an unfulfilled heart. Such a heart will try to squeeze meaning out of people. It will demand attention. It will become easily offended. It will manipulate or isolate. But when the heart is full, it becomes a giver. It releases. It blesses. It supports. It is not possible to fake this for long. Because the fruit will show. A dry soul cannot sustain joy. It will crack under pressure. But a fulfilled heart will keep pouring, even when the cup seems low. Because the Source is not the cup. The Source is God.

When Jesus fed the five thousand, He started with five loaves and two fish. But before multiplying, He gave thanks. That thanksgiving came from a full heart. He was not overwhelmed by the need. He looked up. He gave thanks. Then the miracle flowed. That is the pattern. Fullness first. Then supply.

This is what God wants for His people. He wants sons and daughters who do not measure themselves by the world's scale. He wants hearts that know how to wait, how to rejoice quietly, how to remain steady when nothing changes. That is strength. That is maturity. That is fulfillment.

When someone finds this kind of life, they stop chasing shadows. They stop living for moments. They begin to live from identity. From rest. From assurance. That is where real freedom begins. That is where joy lives. That is the kind of life that brings honor to God. Because it does not just look spiritual. It lives from the Spirit.

FULFILLMENT THAT FLOWS FROM RELATIONSHIP

"When a person walks closely with God, they no longer define themselves by their roles. They find identity in relationship." - Rev Dr. Nadine Nkulu

Fulfillment that flows from relationship with God is the kind that cannot be manufactured, borrowed, or performed into existence. It is the deep satisfaction that springs out of knowing God for who He is, not what He gives. Many people grow up thinking that the Christian life is about checking boxes, attending meetings, fasting on specific days, and trying harder to feel better about themselves. But that cycle often ends with frustration. That is because the soul was not designed to be satisfied by activities. It was designed to be filled through intimacy.

Jesus laid the foundation for this when He told His disciples,

"My meat is to do the will of him that sent me, and to finish his work" in John 4:34.

He was not talking about physical food. He was talking about the nourishment of obedience that comes from a life rooted in relationship with the Father. That means there is something about being close to God that feeds the soul. He did not say His joy was in performing for His Father. He said His fulfillment was in doing the will of the One He loved. Obedience was not a job. It was the fruit of closeness.

In the same chapter, He had just finished speaking with the Samaritan woman at the well. She came with a bucket, but He came with a well. She was trying to draw water, but He offered her living water. And He said,

"Whosoever drinketh of the water that I shall give him shall never thirst" (John 4:14).

That is fulfillment. A place where thirst ends. A place where striving stops. A place where peace is not a visitor but a resident.

Some serve in churches every week, lead others in programs, teach classes, and yet feel empty inside. That is because fulfillment does not flow from titles. It flows from time spent. It is not in how many people they help, but in how deeply they remain connected to the One who helps them. Without abiding, there is no lasting joy. Without intimacy, there is no genuine strength.

In John chapter 15, Jesus taught this clearly. He said in verse 5,

"I am the vine, ye are the branches: He that abideth in me, and I in him, the same bringeth forth much fruit: for without me ye can do nothing."

This was not a suggestion. It was a spiritual law. The branch cannot produce fruit because it works harder. It produces fruit because it stays connected. Fulfillment is the same. It does not come because one tries harder. It comes because one abides deeper.

Abiding is about staying. It is about leaning. It is about continuing in close communion. That is how fulfillment grows. It does not grow in a schedule. It grows in surrender. It is not maintained by effort, but by intimacy.

There is also a danger in thinking that a busy Christian life is equivalent to a fulfilled Christian life. A person can be highly active and still feel distant. That is because motion does not equal connection. The prodigal son, in Luke 15, had to come back to the father before he could be clothed, fed, and celebrated. Until he returned, he was still a son, but he was not enjoying the benefits of sonship.

In the same way, a believer who is always doing but rarely sitting is missing out on the nourishment that comes from relationship. The older brother in that same story stayed home, but still did not enjoy the father. He said,

"Lo, these many years do I serve thee, neither transgressed I at any time thy commandment: and yet thou never gavest me a kid" (Luke 15:29).

He was faithful in service but disconnected in relationship. That shows again that fulfillment is not found solely in service. It flows from closeness.

When a person walks closely with God, they no longer define themselves by their roles. They find identity in relationship. They are not fathers first, or preachers first, or employees first. They are sons and daughters first. And that identity, when nurtured daily in quietness and truth, becomes the foundation for a life that is whole.

A life rooted in relationship with God is not shaken by applause or silence. It is not driven by the need to be seen or celebrated. It is anchored in the joy of being known by God. That is why Jesus said in Matthew 6:6, "But thou, when thou prayest, enter into thy closet, and when thou hast shut thy door, pray to thy Father which is in secret." The secret place is where fulfillment flows. It is where approval is received before performance begins. It is where identity is settled before the day starts.

The person who learns to live from that place is not moved by comparison. They are not trying to measure their walk by what others do. They have tasted and seen that the Lord is good. They are not living for likes. They are living from love.

And that is the turning point. Fulfillment does not come from being celebrated. It comes from being close. When relationship becomes the well, joy becomes the overflow.

THE FRUIT OF WALKING WITH GOD DAILY

"There is a marked difference between those who visit God occasionally and those who walk with Him daily. One lives on borrowed strength; the other lives on a continuous flow." - Rev Dr. Nadine Nkulu

Moments may inspire, but walking daily with God is what transforms. In today's world, where everything is urgent, loud, and fleeting, walking slowly, quietly, and consistently with God feels almost abnormal. But that is where true fruit grows. The soul was not made to run from one emotional high to another. It was made to be rooted, grounded, and nourished.

Micah 6:8 shows what God desires: not spectacular performances or dramatic displays, but a humble walk. The verse reads, "What doth the Lord require of thee, but to do justly, and to love mercy, and to walk humbly with thy God?" There is a pace in walking. It is not fast. It is not impressive to the watching eye. But it is real. Walking humbly is not an act of weakness. It is a life that has decided to take God seriously enough to follow Him step by step, not just in worship settings, but in conversations, decisions, relationships, and daily thoughts.

This walk with God is not an event. It is a way of life. It happens when no one sees. It is practiced in silent mornings, long commutes, evening reflections, and even in painful disappointments. Those who walk with God are not necessarily loud about it, but their lives show it. They do not have to announce their spiritual depth. The fruit announces it for them.

In Galatians 5 verses 22 to 23, Paul wrote that,

"But the fruit of the Spirit is love, joy, peace, longsuffering, gentleness, goodness, faith, meekness, temperance."

He does not refer to these as the rewards of great ministries or the gifts of spiritual offices. He calls them fruit. And fruit does not grow overnight. It grows from a seed that stays. From a root that holds. From a tree that remains. These qualities do not come from trying harder. They come from walking longer.

Love grows when someone keeps walking with God long enough to begin seeing people the way He sees them. Joy grows when the soul has walked through seasons with God and found Him enough every single time. Peace becomes steady when a person learns, through the dailiness of communion, that God is never late and never absent. Long-suffering, or patience, is not built in a prayer line. It is built through walking with God through times that feel like delay, and yet refusing to walk away.

In Genesis 5:24, it says of Enoch,

"And Enoch walked with God: and he was not; for God took him."

This is one of the most profound summaries of a life in the entire Bible. No miracles are recorded for Enoch. No grand speeches. No great buildings or battles. But God thought enough of that man's quiet walk to interrupt the laws of death and take him directly. That shows something eternal happens in the soul of the one who walks with God daily. Fulfillment is not just found; it becomes the environment. And that walk changes everything.

There is something powerful in the dailiness of this walk. In Deuteronomy 8:3, Moses reminded Israel that God humbled them, allowed them to hunger, and fed them with manna,

"that he might make thee know that man doth not live by bread only, but by every word that proceedeth out of the mouth of the Lord."

The manna did not fall once a month. It came daily. They had to trust that each morning, God would provide for them. That process was not just about food. It was about forming a rhythm. A relationship. An unbroken conversation.

Those who walk with God daily begin to lose the appetite for spiritual extremes. They no longer chase events. They desire encounters, but not the kind that shake buildings. The kind that strengthens roots. Because fruit is not loud, it is lasting.

Many people want the results of a strong walk with God, but not the rhythm that accompanies it. They want peace, but not the quietness that produces it. They want joy, but not the obedience that sustains it. They want identity, but not the surrender that forms it. But the fruit of the Spirit is not produced in a rush. It is formed by steady agreement with God; choosing Him again and again, every morning, every decision, every reaction.

In John 15:4, Jesus said,

"Abide in me, and I in you. As the branch cannot bear fruit of itself, except it abide in the vine."

That means staying. That means waking up and choosing again to be His. To hear Him. To please Him. And in the hidden consistency, fruit appears. Not immediately. But certainly.

The peace that grows from walking with God daily is not surface-level. It is not the kind of peace that depends on quiet environments or ideal conditions. It is the peace that kept Paul singing in prison. It is the peace that helped Jesus sleep in a storm. It is the peace that made Stephen kneel and pray for his killers. That kind of peace does not grow in public. It is the fruit of a private, consistent, unshaken walk.

And the joy that comes from that walk is not the temporary laughter that fades when bills come or storms rise. It is the joy that sustains through tears. Like Habakkuk, who said,

"Yet I will rejoice in the Lord, I will joy in the God of my salvation" (Habakkuk 3:18).

Even after writing about loss and chaos. That kind of joy never expires. Because it is not tied to blessings, it is tied to belonging.

Walking with God daily also shapes identity. In a culture that defines people by numbers, applause, and image, it is easy to forget who one is. But in the daily walk with God, the believer is reminded that they are a son. A daughter. Chosen. Loved. Sent. Not because of achievement, but because of adoption. Romans 8:15 says,

"Ye have received the Spirit of adoption, whereby we cry, Abba, Father."

That cry is not learned in crowds. It is learned in the walk. The more a person walks with God, the more they begin to see like Him, feel like Him, and respond like Him. It becomes harder to live in bitterness, easier to forgive, slower to react, quicker to trust. Because the fruit is forming. It is not an act. It is a nature. And that transformation is often quiet.

Abraham walked with God and became a friend of God. That friendship was not built in a day. It was built in a journey, one where Abraham often did not know where he was going, but he knew who he was following. That kind of faith only grows by walking. When Abraham faced the test with Isaac in Genesis 22, he did not panic. He walked up the mountain. He trusted. And fruit appeared in the form of obedience, surrender, and divine provision.

Walking with God daily also changes how one handles suffering. Those who walk with God learn that valleys are not signs of absence but invitations for deeper nearness. David wrote,

"Yea, though I walk through the valley of the shadow of death, I will fear no evil: for thou art with me" (Psalm 23 verse 4).

He did not say he ran through it. He walked. That means he moved slowly, carefully, with God. And even in that dark place, peace remained. Because fruit does not fall off in storms. If it is real, it stays.

In the book *The Believer's Authority,* Kenneth Hagin shared how years of walking with God had trained him not only in hearing God's voice but also in recognizing God's patterns. He noted how many believers are chasing spiritual explosions while missing the gentle whispers that come from consistency. Walking daily with God sharpens that awareness. It tunes the heart to heaven's rhythm.

And when that walk becomes the lifestyle, the fruit becomes undeniable. Those who walk with God daily begin to carry an atmosphere of peace. They do not have to quote scriptures to prove they are filled. The peace in their eyes, the patience in their tone, the gentleness in their dealings, all speak louder than words.

Walking with God daily also means being willing to be corrected. Hebrews 12:6 says,

"For whom the Lord loveth he chasteneth."

The daily walk is not just about comfort. It is also about pruning. And pruning is how fruit remains healthy. A person who refuses correction cannot bear lasting fruit. But one who walks with God learns to see discipline as love, and correction as direction.

There is a significant difference between the man who walks with God daily and the man who only visits God when convenient. One grows fruit. The other seeks flashes. One has roots. The other survives on emotion. And time always reveals which one a person has built.

This is the invitation: not to do more, but to stay longer. Not to rush ahead, but to walk slowly. To take each step with God. To turn devotion into lifestyle. To make silence with Him a daily appointment. To let the Word be daily bread, not a weekend snack. And in doing so, to discover that real fulfillment is not an achievement. It is a consequence of the walk.

The crowd may not celebrate this kind of life. But it is known in heaven. The Father sees. The Spirit bears witness. And the fruit remains.

DISCUSSION QUESTIONS

1.   What does it mean to live with a "fulfilled heart," and how does this differ from seeking fulfillment from external circumstances?

2.   How does the Shunammite woman in 2 Kings 4 demonstrate contentment and a fulfilled heart? What can we learn from her response?

3.   Why is it dangerous to measure our walk with God by visible results, applause, or dramatic experiences? How can we cultivate a heart that finds fulfillment before results?

4.   What are practical ways to "walk with God daily" rather than only visiting Him occasionally? How does consistency in quiet intimacy produce lasting fruit?

5.   How does living from a fulfilled heart free us from the pressure to prove ourselves or compete with others? Can you share a time when you experienced peace from this mindset?

6.   In John 15:4-5, Jesus says a branch produces fruit by abiding in the vine. How does this analogy help us understand that fulfillment comes from staying connected to God rather than striving harder?

7.   How does fulfillment through relationship with God change the way we see ourselves and interact with others? How can this perspective prevent us from using people to meet our own needs?

Chapter Ten

STAYING IN
THE LIGHT

The moment you come into relationship with Christ, you are given access to the light, but you are also expected to live in it."
- Rev. Dr. Nadine Nkulu

When we examine John 3:20-21, we will gain a better understanding of what it means for us to remain in the light. It says that those who do evil hate the light because they do not want their deeds to be exposed. That alone shows that the light is not just a religious word; it is a place of confrontation. A place where the things you hide inside are brought to view. It is no surprise that many claim to love God but secretly avoid His light. They love His power but are afraid of His presence. The light is not just a place where God shines outwardly; it is where He searches inwardly.

Many have been in situations where they professed love for God with their words, but their actions contradicted their words. It may have been lust, pride, dishonesty, envy, or bitterness. They tried to cover it by quoting scripture or serving more in church. But all along, they were growing comfortable in the shadows. That was not staying in the light. That was living in religious performance. Real light does not work like that.

Paul wrote in Romans 13:12 that we should cast off the works of darkness and put on the armor of light. The use of the word armor suggests that the light is not soft or weak. It is a form of protection. But more than that, it is part of our spiritual identity. In other words, the moment you come into relationship with Christ, you are given access to the light, but you are also expected to live in it. You are expected to stay there even when your own flaws make you want to run. The believer who remains in the light is not the one who never sins, but the one who always returns quickly.

One of the easiest ways to lose the presence of God is by pretending before Him. God does not deal with pretense. He is full of mercy, but He only gives that mercy to those who acknowledge their need for it. Proverbs 28:13 makes it clear:

"He that covereth his sins shall not prosper: but whoso confesseth and forsaketh them shall have mercy."

That is what staying in the light looks like. It is a lifestyle of confession. Not a weekly confession in a booth. But a posture of daily openness before God.

Many Christians today do not walk in boldness because they are carrying secret weights. Some have developed spiritual masks that they wear in public. Smiles during worship. Loud prayers. Strong posts online. But when they are alone, they are filled with guilt, anxiety, and shame. That happens when people love the feeling of church more than the light of God. Staying in the light will sometimes break your pride. It will reveal who you truly are. It will bring tears. It may show that you are not as strong as you claimed to be. But that is the point. The light does not shame. It heals.

David is a perfect example. He was a man who made deep mistakes. He committed adultery. He orchestrated murder. Yet he found his way back to God, not by pretending he did nothing wrong, but by stepping into the light. In Psalm 51, he cried,

"Against thee, thee only, have I sinned, and done this evil in thy sight."

That was not a public speech. It was a personal cry. That was what kept him in the light, even after his failure. He chose exposure over cover-up.

Staying in the light is the opposite of hiding. And hiding is not just running physically. It can also be mental and emotional. Adam and Eve ate the fruit in Genesis 3. The moment their eyes were opened, they ran and hid. But what did God say? He called out, "Where art thou?" That was the first evidence of the light calling man. And even then, instead of coming clean, they gave reasons and blamed each other. The moment blame enters, the light begins to fade.

The one who lives in the light does not wait for God to ask where he is. He comes forward quickly. He admits fault. He welcomes correction. He refuses to live by double standards. That is the difference between Saul and David. Both sinned. But one shifted responsibility; the other took ownership. Staying in the light does not mean you are perfect. It means you are accountable. It means you take responsibility without excuses.

The armor of light is not something you put on when things are going well. In fact, the times when you feel most tempted to sin are the times when you need to stay in the light the most. Some people run from God when they fall. They stop praying. They stop reading scripture. They avoid their mentors or spiritual friends. That is a sign that they are slipping into the shadows. The shadows may feel safer, but they are not. They are the breeding ground for spiritual dryness.

When a person stops responding to conviction, it is a sign that they have stepped away from the light. They may still attend church. They may still give. But the inner sharpness is gone. They no longer feel sorrow over sin. They justify it. They call it weakness instead of wickedness. That is what happens when light is reduced to religion. People begin to measure their walk with God by activity instead of intimacy.

Some try to escape the light by surrounding themselves with others who are in the dark. That way, they feel less convicted. They find comfort in numbers. But that comfort is false. Light is not measured by how many agree with you. It is measured by how closely you are walking with Christ. The standard is not your circle. It is the Word of God.

Many lives have been destroyed because they rejected the discipline of the light. They chose applause over truth. They preferred good feelings over deep convictions. And as a result, their walk with God became shallow. Staying in the light will cost you your pride. But it will give you your purity. It will break your ego. But it will build your spirit.

Jesus said in John 8:12,

"I am the light of the world: he that followeth me shall not walk in darkness, but shall have the light of life."

That means the closer you walk with Him, the more you see clearly. Things that used to feel normal will begin to feel wrong. Places that used to excite you will no longer have that power. That is what the light does. It shifts your taste.

GUARDING YOUR CONNECTION

"Just like passwords are protected and wallets are secured, the soul must be treated with care. The heart must be guarded because it is easily influenced." - Rev Dr. Nadine Nkulu

After a person steps into the light and chooses to remain there, the next most crucial decision is to guard what has been found. Spiritual connection is not like a photograph that gets saved permanently; it is more like a living fire that must be kept burning. It is not the initial experience that sustains a believer, but the continued feeding of the fire within. Many who once walked in close proximity to God slowly lost that intimacy, not because they hated God, but because they did not guard it.

Leviticus 6:12-13 gives a physical picture of a spiritual principle. The fire on the altar had to be fed every morning. It was not left to chance. The priest had a responsibility. He was not told to light it once and walk away. The instruction was clear.

"The fire shall ever be burning upon the altar; it shall never go out.

That verse is both a command and a warning. It shows that even God-given fire will go out if neglected.

Spiritual connection is not a one-time deposit; it is a daily investment. Some began with passion: waking up early, praying with a hunger for God, and reading scripture with joy. But over time, the fire weakened. Not because God left them, but because the altar was not maintained. The priest added wood every morning.

In the same way, time with God is the wood. Worship is the wood. Quiet surrender is the wood. The moment these are neglected, the fire begins to dim.

Many believers fall into this silent drift. They remember how it used to be; how they used to feel God deeply, how they wept during worship, how they could not go a day without seeking Him. But now, that passion feels distant. The distance did not happen overnight. It came little by little. A few missed prayers. A few compromises. A few distractions. That is how drift begins. Slowly. Almost unnoticeable.

Solomon is one of the most tragic stories in Scripture. He loved God. He was blessed with wisdom. He built the temple. He prayed publicly. Yet 1 Kings 11:4 reveals that his heart was not fully after the Lord. His drift began with small openings; marriages to women who did not share his faith. These alliances were not just emotional; they were spiritual compromises. They pulled his affection. They divided his loyalty. Eventually, they turned his heart to other gods.

This shows that love for God does not always disappear suddenly. Sometimes, it simply becomes shared. Shared with ambition. Shared with relationships. Shared with personal goals. And once the heart is divided, the connection is weakened. Guarding connection means refusing to allow any other affection to take the place of God. It means refusing to allow substitutes or success to seduce away what belongs only to Him.

A guarded connection requires filters. Just as people protect their devices from viruses and their homes from strangers, the soul must be protected from corrupting influences. What enters the ears affects faith. What the eyes see shapes desire. What the heart meditates on grows stronger. A believer must take responsibility for what enters. This is not legalism. This is survival. The altar must be protected.

One of the greatest enemies of connection is busyness. It is not that people do not want to pray. It is that everything else feels more urgent. Work. Deadlines. Social media. Goals. Over time, what should be first becomes last. What should be daily becomes occasional. And soon, God becomes an option instead of the center. Jesus never said the fire would stay without work. He said in Luke 9:23, "If any man will come after me, let him deny himself daily." Daily. Not occasionally.

Another layer of protection is worship. Not just the songs sung in church, but the posture of reverence. Worship silences noise. It re-centers the soul. It brings back perspective. Worship is not a sound; it is surrender. It is what reminds a person that God is not a background presence, but the only source. The more a person worships, the more sensitive they become. And the more sensitive they are, the easier it is to hear God.

Guarding the connection also includes setting boundaries. Boundaries in relationships. Boundaries in time. Boundaries in habits. Anything that drains affection for God must be questioned. A person cannot spend hours feeding their flesh and expect their spirit to remain on fire. That is unrealistic. Paul wrote in Galatians 6:7,

"Be not deceived; God is not mocked: for whatsoever a man soweth, that shall he also reap."

If you sow to the spirit, you reap life. If you sow to the flesh, you reap corruption.

Many have allowed the fire on their altar to go out because they thought connection was automatic. But no connection is automatic. Even in real life, relationships require nurturing and care. A friendship that is not maintained will fade. A marriage that is not guarded will grow cold. In the same way, a walk with God that is not fed will wither. The fire needs attention.

Some have tried to substitute church attendance for personal devotion. They believe that if they keep serving, the fire will stay. But service without intimacy is a trap. It leads to burnout. It leads to frustration. Martha in Luke 10 was busy serving. But Jesus said Mary had chosen the better part, sitting at His feet. That was not laziness. That was connection.

God is not looking for workers who forget to watch the flame. He is looking for lovers. Lovers who protect their time with Him.

Who fight to stay close. Who recognize when distance is growing and take action to return. A guarded connection is not emotion; it is decision. It is the quiet choice to say no to things that interrupt communion.

HABITS THAT SUSTAIN FULFILLMENT

"Evening prayer closed the day with reflection, surrender, and gratitude." - Rev Dr. Nadine Nkulu

Psalm 55:17 says, "Evening, and morning, and at noon, will I pray, and cry aloud: and he shall hear my voice."

This was not an exaggeration. It was a lived pattern. The psalmist created spiritual pauses throughout the day to re-center his soul. Morning prayer acknowledged the newness of God's mercy. Midday prayer confronted the distractions and burdens of work and people. Evening prayer closed the day with reflection, surrender, and gratitude.

These divine interruptions kept the heart from being swallowed by busyness. They fought against forgetfulness. They broke the day into three holy segments that constantly pointed back to God. In a noisy world, such rhythms have become almost forgotten. Yet they are not optional for a fulfilled life. A believer who desires lasting fulfillment must make room, not just for activities, but for silence, scripture, prayer, and reflection.

One of the first sustaining habits is scripture reading not as information, but for transformation. Many read the Bible to gather knowledge. But knowledge without transformation is deception. James 1:22 says,

"But be ye doers of the word, and not hearers only, deceiving your own selves."

The deception is subtle; it convinces the heart that hearing is enough. But scripture must be read to change the heart. To confront pride. To soften resistance. To feed the soul.

Transformation happens when scripture is approached with humility. Not to find what is agreeable, but to find what is true. Not to defend opinions, but to receive correction.

Another sustaining habit is worship without music. This does not diminish musical worship but reminds us that authentic worship is not limited to sound. Worship is posture. It is reverence. It is deep acknowledgment of God's worthiness. One can worship in silence. One can worship in awe. Worship without music trains the heart to remain low before God, even when there is no emotional atmosphere.

Habakkuk 2:20 says,

"But the Lord is in his holy temple: let all the earth keep silence before him."

That is worship. Not noise. Not movement. Just silence that bows before God. This kind of habit deepens fulfillment because it breaks dependency on feeling. It teaches the soul to honor God without being stirred by music or environment. It creates mature worshipers who do not need a worship leader to lift their hands.

A vital habit that sustains fulfillment is journaling His voice and your journey. Not because God forgets, but because humans do. Journaling creates remembrance. It builds an altar of testimony. It allows a person to go back and see the hand of God when feelings are dry. Journaling also tracks growth. What was once a struggle becomes a testimony. What was once a question becomes a revelation.

Psalm 102:18 says,

"This shall be written for the generation to come: and the people which shall be created shall praise the Lord."

Some things must be written, not for public sharing, but for personal anchoring. Many have drifted because they forgot what God once said. They forgot what He once did. Writing down prayers, revelations, corrections, and lessons helps the heart remain steady and focused. It keeps memory alive.

Another essential habit is fasting, not as a religious ritual, but as a reset. Fasting is not a hunger strike. It is a humbling. It is a way to break fleshly appetites and remind the soul who is in charge. Jesus assumed fasting in Matthew 6. He said, "When ye fast," not if. Fasting makes room. It quiets the body to awaken the spirit. It confronts dependency. It reorders priorities.

Fasting also prepares the heart for deeper intimacy. It clears the fog. It reveals what is truly happening inside. Isaiah 58 provides a comprehensive picture of a fast that pleases God, not just denying food, but also breaking yokes, humbling pride, and loving the needy. A fast with the right heart becomes a spiritual reset. It reignites hunger. It realigns the spirit. And it fuels long-term fulfillment.

Also, Fulfillment is hard to maintain in isolation. Hebrews 10:25 says,

"Not forsaking the assembling of ourselves together.

This is not just about attending services. It is about walking with others who sharpen, encourage, and correct one another. Proverbs 27:17 says,

"Iron sharpeneth iron."

The right relationships fan the flame. They point out drift. They remind a person who they are when identity feels blurred.

But not every community helps. Crowds can distract. The wrong voices can confuse. A fulfilling spiritual life requires relationships that build faith, not flatter the ego. Relationships that confront sin, not comfort dysfunction. Accountability is not legalism. It is protection. People grow in honesty, not in hiding. Sharing struggles, asking for help, and celebrating victories —all of it matters. Those who hide do not heal.

Lastly, a habit that sustains fulfillment is giving without seeking recognition. Giving keeps the heart unselfish. It pushes against the culture of entitlement. It turns the focus outward. Acts 20:35 says,

"It is more blessed to give than to receive."

When a person becomes generous with time, resources, and encouragement, they remain aligned with God's nature. God is a giver. Those who imitate Him in this way stay fresh. They do not become bitter or isolated.

The habits that sustain fulfillment are not complicated. But they are costly. They cost time, attention, and effort. They require saying no to good things to say yes to the best things. They require consistency. And they are often built in secret, not in the spotlight. The goal is not to be admired. The goal is to remain in step with God.

There will be days when emotions are low, when life is confusing, when prayers seem dry. However, the person who has developed habits will persist. They do not wait for lightning; they keep the lamp burning. And in that quiet, consistent walk, fulfillment is not only found but preserved. Because the soul was not built to live off moments; it was built to grow through patterns. Patterns shaped by love. Sustained by grace, and guarded by habits that last.

CONCLUSION
I AM COMING OUT OF THE SHADOWS

As we have seen in this book, the shadows are not just dark spaces where we hide from the world. They are places where we forget who we are, where we lose our joy, and where the presence of God becomes distant. The journey through this book has not been easy, but it has been necessary. We have exposed the things we often avoid. We have faced truths that are easier left buried. And now, we have reached a point where running is no longer an option. This is the moment of return.

I don't want this conclusion to resemble an emotional goodbye; rather, it is a profound and sober declaration. It is a vow that says, I refuse to remain hidden. I refuse to stay numb. I refuse to live as if I were not created for God. I am coming out of the shadows. Not just to be seen by people, but to walk again with the One who has always seen me. This is not a step back into activity. It is a step forward into intimacy.

Earlier in this book, we learned that shadows can appear to be distractions. They can resemble pain that has not been fully healed. They can even look like ministry, performance, and religious routine. But whatever shape they take, one thing remains the same. The shadows always replace the presence of God with something else. That something may not be inherently evil, but it slowly takes the place of God in our hearts.

The problem is not just that we drifted. The issue is that we allowed the drift to continue. But now, the mercy of God is calling us back. He is not shouting. He is not angry. He is speaking in a voice of remembrance. A voice that says, I still know who you are. I still see who I created you to be.

As we read in Jeremiah chapter three, verses twelve to fourteen:

"Return, thou backsliding Israel, saith the Lord. I will not cause mine anger to fall upon you. For I am merciful, saith the Lord, and I will not keep anger for ever. Only acknowledge thine iniquity. Return, O backsliding children, saith the Lord. For I am married unto you."

This is not the voice of a disappointed boss. This is the cry of a Father. The One who never stopped waiting. He is not asking us to return to church attendance alone. He is not asking us to return to duty or service. He is calling us back to Himself. This is the difference. Coming out of the shadows means returning to Him, not just returning to what we used to do.

Earlier in this book, we remembered Adam in the garden. He walked with God in the cool of the day. That was before there was sin. Before there was work. Before there was church. What existed was relationship. That is what the shadows tried to erase from our memory. But now we remember again. We were made to walk with God. We were made to know Him. We were made for face-to-face friendship, not survival.

Here is what makes the shadows so deceptive. They offer a false version of fulfillment. They tell us that success will satisfy. They tell us that performance is enough. They make us chase approval, applause, and outcomes, thinking those things will fill the void inside. But they never do. They make us feel busy, but never full. They make us look powerful, but feel empty. They feed the outer life while starving the inner one. That is what many of us have done. We tried to fill the ache in our hearts with shadows. Shadows of ambition. Shadows of busyness. Shadows of religious activity. Even shadows of ministry. But as we have clearly seen in this book, what we were truly longing for all along was not results; it was relationship. Not noise; but nearness. Not pressure; but presence.

We must admit now that shadows are not always obvious. They hide behind good things. But they are still substitutes. And substitutes never satisfy. Only God can satisfy the soul. Only intimacy with Him can provide the kind of fulfillment that reaches deep and remains steady.

Many of us who have read this book have served. We have given.

We have obeyed. But along the way, something went quiet inside. We stopped feeling. We stopped burning. We started to live on autopilot. But now, we know that numbness is not normal. We know that living distant from God, even if we are doing spiritual things, is not our true life.

So, this moment is not about shame. It is about decision. It is about recognizing that something has to change. The truth is, we have tried to do it our own way. We have tried to push through pain without healing. We have tried to keep going without being honest. But as we said earlier, God does not restore us by force. He invites us with love.

This is your invitation. Not tomorrow. Not when you feel ready. But now. It is time to say with all honesty and all clarity, I am coming out of the shadows.

I am no longer comfortable with being half-alive. I am no longer satisfied with empty prayers. I am no longer pretending that I am close to God when I know I am far. This is not about emotions. This is about truth. This is about turning back, not just to a better season, but to the presence of God Himself.

Some may feel that it is too late. That too much damage has been done. But we must remember, as we saw in earlier chapters, that God does not work according to our shame. He works by mercy. If you still feel a pull in your heart, that means His hand is still reaching for you. The shadows may have convinced you that God stopped looking for you. But He never left. Even when you stopped praying. Even when you turned your back. He stayed.

This moment of coming out will require courage. You may need to step away from certain patterns. You may need to talk to someone. You may need to create space for silence again. This is not about being impressive. It is about being real. Some of us will need to start by simply sitting in a room alone and saying, God, I miss You. That is a powerful prayer. That is the beginning of restoration.

To come out of the shadows is to choose life. Not the life of busy routine, but the life of deep connection. It is to say, I want my joy back. I want my peace back. I want to love God again the way I did before I got distracted. This is not a desire that comes from human strength. It is the Spirit of God stirring you to return.

As Tozer wrote in *The Pursuit of God*, "When the heart begins to hunger for God, that is the proof that God has already made the first move." He always starts the process of returning. We simply respond.

So let us respond. Let us not harden our hearts. Let us not delay. Say it aloud. Write it down if you must.

I am coming out of the shadows. I will not settle for distance. I will not live on secondhand faith. I will not continue empty. I will return to the secret place. I will pursue God again. I will believe again. I will burn again.

I will not chase shadows. I will not look to substitutes. I will seek the face of God. I will live for His presence. Because only there will I be whole.

This is the final word, but it is also your new beginning. The light is ahead of you. The Father is waiting. The shadows have lost. You are rising. You are remembering. You are returning.

Welcome back to the presence. Welcome back to intimacy. Welcome back to fulfillment. Welcome back to who you were always meant to be.

DISCUSSION QUESTIONS

1. The text says, "The moment you come into relationship with Christ, you are given access to the light, but you are also expected to live in it." What does it mean to you personally to "live in the light" rather than just have access to it?

2. In John 3:20-21, the light exposes what is hidden in our hearts. Can you identify areas in your life where you might be avoiding God's light? How can you take steps to face them?

3. The author emphasizes confession and daily openness to God as a lifestyle, not a weekly activity. How can we practically cultivate this habit of ongoing confession and transparency with God?

4. Worship, scripture reading, journaling, fasting, and fellowship are described as habits that sustain fulfillment. Which of these habits do you currently practice consistently, and which could you strengthen to guard your connection with God?

5. The author contrasts Adam and Eve hiding after sin with David's confession in Psalm 51. How does humility and ownership of our mistakes help us remain in the light?

6. Relationships are said to sharpen and protect our spiritual walk. How have your friends or small group members helped you stay close to God? How can you support each other in guarding your connection with God?

7. Finally, the author calls for a conscious decision: "I am coming out of the shadows." What specific steps can you take this week to step out of any spiritual shadows and pursue intimacy with God?

BIBLIOGRAPHY
1. A.W. Tozer – *The Pursuit of God*
2. Brother Lawrence – *The Practice of the Presence of God*
3. Dallas Willard – *The Spirit of the Disciplines: Understanding How God Changes Lives*
4. Richard J. Foster – *Celebration of Discipline: The Path to Spiritual Growth*
5. Henry Blackaby & Claude King – *Experiencing God: Knowing and Doing the Will of God*
6. John Bevere – *The Bait of Satan: Living Free from the Deadly Trap of Offense*
7. Watchman Nee – *The Normal Christian Life*
8. Francis Chan – *Crazy Love: Overwhelmed by a Relentless God*
9. Leonard Ravenhill – *Why Revival Tarries*
10. Andrew Murray – *Absolute Surrender*
11. F.F. Bruce – *The Epistle to the Hebrews: The First Apology for Christianity*
12. Geerhardus Vos – *Biblical Theology: Old and New Testaments*
13. R.C. Sproul – *Knowing Scripture*
14. N.T. Wright – *The New Testament and the People of God*
15. Patrick Fairbairn – *The Typology of Scripture*
16. Neil T. Anderson – *Victory Over the Darkness: Realizing the Power of Your Identity in Christ*
17. Timothy Keller – *Counterfeit Gods: The Empty Promises of Money, Sex, and Power, and the Only Hope that Matters*
18. Paul David Tripp – *New Morning Mercies: A Daily Gospel Devotional*
19. Andrew Wommack – *Spirit, Soul & Body*
20. T. Austin-Sparks – *The Centrality and Supremacy of the Lord Jesus Christ*
21. Oswald Chambers – *My Utmost for His Highest*
22. Martyn Lloyd-Jones – S*piritual Depression: Its Causes and Its Cure*
23. Michael Reeves – *Delighting in the Trinity*
24. C. Peter Wagner – *The Church in the Workplace: How God's People Can Transform Society*

25. Gordon D. Fee – *Paul, the Spirit, and the People of God*
26. Kenneth E. Hagin – *I Believe in Visions*